SIR GEORGE WILLIAMS UNIVERSITY
LIBRARY

Studies in International Education

Planning and educational development in India

JOHN A. LASKA

Institute of International Studies
Teachers College, Columbia University

TEACHERS COLLEGE PRESS
Teachers College, Columbia University
New York, New York

© 1968 by Teachers College Press

Library of Congress Catalog Card No. 68–23784

Manufactured in the United States of America

To my
mother and father

Acknowledgements

This study represents the results of field research conducted in India from August, 1962 to June, 1963, while the author was the holder of a Ford Foundation Foreign Area Training Fellowship. The investigation was undertaken at the initiative of the author and in no way constitutes an official statement of the views of the Ford Foundation.

The study could not have been completed without the generous help provided by the many persons in India from whom advice and data were solicited. In particular, the cooperation of officials in the Union Ministry of Education, Planning Commission, University Grants Commission, and the state departments of education must be acknowledged. The author is also very appreciative of the assistance received from the staffs of the Ford Foundation and the Institute of Applied Manpower Research in New Delhi. Special thanks are due to Mr. Robert Clark, consultant to the Ford Foundation on manpower, for his many kindnesses.

The following professors at Columbia University contributed invaluable criticism and advice during the preparation of the study: C. T. Hu, R. Freeman Butts, Ainslie T. Embree, and David G. Scanlon. For their guidance, inspiration and friendship, the author would like to express his deepest gratitude. They should not, of course, be held responsible for the shortcomings in this work.

JOHN A. LASKA

Foreword

This analysis of the process of educational planning in India is the first of a projected series of Studies in International Education sponsored by the Institute of International Studies of Teachers College, Columbia University. It lays on the academic table for examination and dissection some of the fundamental problems that must be faced by nations in their efforts to use education as an instrument of modernization. It does not praise, nor scold, nor preach, nor prophesy. It does try to provide hard data for the consideration of scholars, practitioners, and policy-makers alike.

Professor Laska began this study while a graduate student at Teachers College, carried it forward in India, and completed it while a Research Associate in the Institute of International Studies. He is dealing with a country whose future is by common consent of first importance to the rest of the world—and a country whose problems are appallingly complex and gigantic. And he is dealing with a process of educational planning that has recently become the lodestar for many educators, economists, and politicians in their search for a secure road to national development. On both counts his subject merits close attention.

In succinct and sometimes staccato fashion, Professor Laska deals with basic theoretical and practical problems. He describes the general structure of Indian education and presents a valuable historical résumé of the major educational plans that have been drawn up in India during the fifteen years that followed independence. Discussions of educational planning and the plans themselves are so often ahistorical in nature that the longitudinal comparison of the successive plans is especially illuminating.

Readers will also find stimulating his theoretical formulation of the three stages of educational development that characterize modernizing nations. If you were a national policy-maker in a traditional nation that desperately needed and wanted to become modern, would you opt for universal primary education before you established new universities or would you choose the reverse? Or some other priority? Professor Laska argues that universities are the very essence of a modern educational system and thus should have highest priority in the first stage of developing a modern system of education. This is an intriguing and not always popular theory. Its application to India's planning efforts will arouse much useful discussion.

Another finding that will be intriguing to planners and educators alike is the disparity discovered between the *stated goals* of the educational plans and the quantitative projections in the plans themselves. Both of these "plans" are found to be at variance with what has actually happened.

Professor Laska does not speculate much about the reasons for these disparities—perhaps not enough—but he has amassed a great deal of informative data that will provide a solid basis for analysis and debate by those who do wish to speculate. More importantly, the data will be useful for those who wish fearlessly to examine the fundamental political and educational dynamics of educational planning and the implementation of educational plans. There are those who will not be too happy with some of Professor Laska's findings, but they will need to reckon with them. He provides a model for dispassionate marshalling of data. The excruciating dilemma involved in deciding whether a nation should press forward toward universal primary education or should establish more universities requires all of the cold light of analysis that can be mustered. This study provides a temperate and tempered means to that end.

R. Freeman Butts
Director
Institute of International Studies
Teachers College, Columbia University

New York
January 3, 1968

Contents

I   *Introduction*

Until about a decade ago, the connection between education and national development had received relatively little public attention. But the spectacular impact of Soviet technological achievements, the belated recognition of the needs of underdeveloped societies for educated manpower as well as capital investment, and the preparation of analyses which purport to show the amount of additional individual and national income that can be attributed to education—all of these have combined to give a new emphasis to the school as a factor in economic and social development.

Paralleling this increased awareness of the importance of education in a modern society is a growing interest in formal national educational planning, as a method for obtaining maximum benefits from the resources available for the school system. Many nations have now either produced educational plans or are attempting to do so.[1] These countries are being encouraged and supported in their efforts by such organizations as UNESCO, the Organization for Economic Cooperation and Development (OECD), the International Bank for Reconstruction and Development (the World Bank), the U.S. Agency for International Development, and the recently founded International Institute for Educational Planning.

This ready acceptance of the technique of formal national educational planning seems to be predicated upon two assumptions: (1) that a plan will be able to indicate "correctly" the type of educational development required, and (2) that the plan, once prepared, will be implemented. Yet it may well be asked to what extent these assumptions are valid. Fortunately, it is not necessary to speculate about the problems which may be encountered in formulating and carrying out educational plans. Because several countries have been engaged in formal national educational planning for a number of years, a body

---

[1] A questionnaire survey undertaken by the International Bureau of Education and UNESCO (1962, p. ix), which obtained replies from more than seventy countries, revealed that two-fifths already had provisions for over-all educational planning and that another one-fifth expected to establish such plans within a short time.

of experience is available which can be consulted for evidence regarding the effectiveness of this technique. The present investigation will seek to provide such evidence based on an examination of the role of planning in India's educational development using data for 1947–1961.

The Nature of Educational Planning

For an understanding of what is meant by educational planning, it is necessary to begin with a definition of terms.[2] A "plan" may be defined as a projected course of action for the accomplishment of an objective. In short, plans relate means to ends. Although for most purposes it is helpful to retain the means-ends dichotomy, it should be recognized that these are only relative concepts. From the standpoint of some ultimate end, all actions that contribute to the attainment of the objective are means. However, these means may also be regarded as ends from the point of view of the actions which are in turn necessary for their accomplishment. Thus the educational outcomes sought in an educational plan are at once both ends and means: they are the objectives which it is the purpose of the plan to achieve, but they are also the means to some further end.

"Education" may be defined as the management of learning experiences in order to bring about desired changes in human behavior. Defined in this way, "education" is more inclusive than "schooling," since it would also encompass informal instruction, such as a parent teaching a child. In the present study, however, following customary usage, "education" will be regarded as equivalent to "schooling," and the expression "educational system" will be used synonymously with "school system." Because the schools are usually susceptible to control by the entire society, they serve as its major instrument for the achievement of educational tasks that are being inadequately or less efficiently fulfilled by other educational agencies.

The conclusion that emerges from the joint consideration of these two terms is that all education must be planned, since education has been defined as a purposeful activity directed toward the accomplishment of a specified learning objective. In any society with a school system, a large number of educational plans presumably exist: those of students, their parents, and their teachers, and those of school authorities and the government officials in charge of the educational system. With planning activities so broadly diffused, only a part of the planning within a school system can be expected to involve the

[2] As yet, few attempts have been made to provide a conceptual analysis of the process of educational planning. However, see C. Arnold Anderson and Mary Jean Bowman (1964, pp. 4–46).

I   *Introduction*

Until about a decade ago, the connection between education and national development had received relatively little public attention. But the spectacular impact of Soviet technological achievements, the belated recognition of the needs of underdeveloped societies for educated manpower as well as capital investment, and the preparation of analyses which purport to show the amount of additional individual and national income that can be attributed to education—all of these have combined to give a new emphasis to the school as a factor in economic and social development.

Paralleling this increased awareness of the importance of education in a modern society is a growing interest in formal national educational planning, as a method for obtaining maximum benefits from the resources available for the school system. Many nations have now either produced educational plans or are attempting to do so.[1] These countries are being encouraged and supported in their efforts by such organizations as UNESCO, the Organization for Economic Cooperation and Development (OECD), the International Bank for Reconstruction and Development (the World Bank), the U.S. Agency for International Development, and the recently founded International Institute for Educational Planning.

This ready acceptance of the technique of formal national educational planning seems to be predicated upon two assumptions: (1) that a plan will be able to indicate "correctly" the type of educational development required, and (2) that the plan, once prepared, will be implemented. Yet it may well be asked to what extent these assumptions are valid. Fortunately, it is not necessary to speculate about the problems which may be encountered in formulating and carrying out educational plans. Because several countries have been engaged in formal national educational planning for a number of years, a body

[1] A questionnaire survey undertaken by the International Bureau of Education and UNESCO (1962, p. ix), which obtained replies from more than seventy countries, revealed that two-fifths already had provisions for over-all educational planning and that another one-fifth expected to establish such plans within a short time.

1

system as a whole, and much of this may be informal. Yet it is equally evident that most countries—those having some measure of central control or influence over their schools—must also have national educational planning, fragmentary and inchoate as it may be.

A society may, of course, decide to forsake the possible benefits of more complete central control of the educational system in deference to other values. The traditional freedom allotted to the university is an example of such a partial renunciation of control by society. Also, in some countries, private bodies may be granted a large amount of freedom in the management of educational institutions, while under a federal system of government the constituent states may be accorded considerable autonomy in the administration of schools. But the desirability of exercising at least some degree of unitary societal direction over the educational system is not, in most countries, a major issue.[3]

The basic justification for planning is the contribution that it can make to the more efficient use of resources. If prior rational consideration is given to the choice of a goal and the means for its achievement, a more efficient course of action should be the result. An optimal plan would be one which maximized the attainment of desired ends. For the preparation of such a plan, however, it would be necessary to possess (1) full knowledge of all possible courses of action, (2) full knowledge of the consequences that would follow from each alternative, and (3) a complete preference-ordering for each of these consequences.[4] Since information of this completeness is clearly impossible to obtain in the real world, the costs of attempting to overcome the limitations on human knowledge operate as a fundamental constraint on the amount of effort that can be devoted to planning and the degree of optimality that can be achieved.

Given this situation, a national educational plan that is only *relatively optimal* must be the desideratum. The process by which such a plan is produced should fulfill two requirements. First, the expenditures on the planning process should have a marginal cost which equals the marginal benefits gained from the resulting improvement in the efficiency of the planned action (here, as elsewhere in this study, benefits and costs are considered to include non-pecuniary advantages and disadvantages). Although difficult to calculate in practice, this requirement merely stipulates that the resources available for educational development should be allocated between planning and implementation in such a manner that maximum net benefits are obtained.

As a second requirement, the procedures employed in the plan-

[3] For an argument in favor of only minimal government control over the schools, see Milton Friedman (1962, pp. 85–107).

[4] Adapted from James G. March and Herbert A. Simon (1958, pp. 137–141).

ning process—which may be called the "technology" of planning—should, for the particular circumstances of the nation concerned, reflect the "current state of the art." A given technology of educational planning is representative of the current state of the art to the extent that it utilizes the most efficient procedures available. Compared with technologies in the area of material production, it is more difficult to measure objectively the performance of an educational planning technology. Nevertheless, it seems no less appropriate to regard planning as a production process, in which inputs of labor are transformed with the use of relevant procedures into a finished plan.[5]

It might appear that a relatively optimal plan—once formulated—would always be implemented, for the plan by definition would specify a desirable objective and an adequate means for its attainment. But the fact that a relatively optimal plan has been prepared does not mean that the course of action indicated will actually be carried out: a plan is not a prediction. All plans entail a contingency; a plan in effect states that if certain actions are accomplished, certain results will follow. Consequently, before the goal of a plan can be achieved, it is necessary that the plan be accepted as a basis for action. For a national educational plan, this acceptance would ordinarily take place at the level of the national government.

The possibility exists, therefore, that an educational plan may be unacceptable to the national government, or if ostensibly adopted as national policy, may not in fact be carried out. In considering the actual process of educational planning in a society, two questions thus appear to be critical: can a relatively optimal educational plan be formulated, and can such a plan be implemented?

Purpose of the Study

Using India as a case study, it will be the purpose of this investigation to determine whether that country has been able to prepare and execute a relatively optimal national educational plan. India would seem to be a particularly good choice for a case study. Of all the countries outside the Communist bloc, it has been one of the most devoted to the concept of national planning. India has had formal national educational planning since its attainment of independence in 1947, and thus in 1961 represented a country with nearly fifteen years of experience in the utilization of this technique.

[5] A similar view of the planning process has been taken by Jan Tinbergen (1964, pp. 49–50), who considers planning as "one of the productive activities of an economy." Therefore, "as with any economic activity, planning should be carried on to the point where marginal revenue equals marginal cost."

This analysis is not intended to be an examination of the various causal factors involved in the planning process. A more immediate requirement, it would seem, is simply to ascertain whether effective national educational planning is feasible. After this has been accomplished, later investigations concerned with causal relationships can be undertaken to explore the reasons for success or failure. The emphasis, therefore, will be on what has been achieved in India through educational planning, and not how or why.

Although several authorities have stressed the importance of implementation for effective planning,[6] the necessity of considering implementation in conjunction with an assessment of the optimality of the plan has not been so widely recognized. Yet it would seem impossible to analyze the significance of plan implementation or non-implementation without assessing the optimality of the plan. The execution of an inappropriate plan, for example, would be clearly undesirable. Those who would emphasize implementation as the sole or principal criterion of effective planning also seem to be ignoring the fact that the educational systems of most countries are guided by at least informal plans; as indicated above, some kind of planning is implicit in the carrying out of all educational activities. The basic problem confronting the national educational planners, therefore, is not to obtain the implementation of any plan, but rather to insure that the most suitable plan is put into effect.

Limitations of the Study

The following limitations on the scope of the present investigation are essential in order to permit the required assessment of the optimality of India's educational plans and the measurement of their implementation. This study will be confined to the analysis of formal national educational plans, since it is the technique of formal planning which is the focus of current interest. A formal national plan is defined as one which has been produced by an individual or organization legitimately entitled to do so on behalf of the society; it exists in documentary form and is readily identifiable as a plan. It is further assumed that such plan documents may be regarded as constituting "finished plans," after which the task is one of implementation.

To be identified as an educational plan, a document would need to indicate the basic educational goals that are to be achieved (the means to the ultimate ends of the society); it may also prescribe the principal means to be employed in attaining the basic goals. How-

[6] See, for example, Frederick Harbison and Charles A. Myers (1964, pp. 222–223) and Beresford Hayward (1964, pp. 82–102).

ever, it cannot be expected that a plan will afford a detailed statement of means. Apart from the costs which this would entail, the quality of the plan would also suffer, owing to its becoming too prescriptive and inflexible. Moreover, once goals of a certain specificity have been established, it is not always necessary to stipulate the means, if it is assumed that procedures already exist which may be used to reach the goals. As a minimum, therefore, an educational plan would have to specify the following two objectives: *how much* education of *what kind* is to be provided. The plan might also state *to whom* this education is to be given, *where*, and *by what means*, but these stipulations could be omitted if they were regarded as means to be decided upon by the implementing agency, rather than as goals. The two basic objectives, however, could not be left out without rendering the plan meaningless.

In order to facilitate the assessment of optimality and the measurement of implementation that are essential for this investigation, India's educational plans will be examined with respect to only one of the two primary goals: the determination of *how much* education should be provided. Although this is fundamentally a quantitative problem, it is impossible to separate quantity from quality; a given amount of schooling must refer to a particular kind of schooling. To this extent, therefore, it will always be necessary to include the qualitative factor. There are three reasons for this limitation. First, it is believed that the optimality of an educational plan can best be analyzed with reference to quantitative rather than qualitative goals. Second, the achievement of an objective that is quantitatively expressed is relatively easy to ascertain; the attainment of a qualitative goal, on the other hand, is much more difficult to measure. And third, there is a need to demonstrate the importance of such statistical measures as completion ratios in the analysis of educational development: in spite of the convenience of using statistical data—and the fact that educational phenomena are as much quantitative as they are qualitative—statistics have been little utilized for the study of national school systems.[7]

It must be stressed that there is no wholly satisfactory method for determining the optimality of an educational plan—a situation that is inherent in the completeness of the knowledge required for a relatively optimal plan. For the purposes of the present study, therefore, only a limited interpretation of optimality will be employed. This interpretation could make use of either the two criteria for relative optimality or the three criteria for optimality presented above. Because of the difficulty of assessing whether the expenditures on educational planning in India resulted in a marginal cost equal to the marginal

[7] See John A. Laska (1965).

benefits obtained, and because an evaluation of the technology of planning would in any case entail a consideration of the capability of the planners to deal effectively with the three criteria for optimality, it will be more convenient to analyze India's educational plans with respect to these three criteria—on the assumption that a plan which approaches optimality is also one that meets the criteria for relative optimality. However, in order to apply the three criteria for optimality, several additional simplifying assumptions will be necessary.

One set of simplifying assumptions is related to the first criterion for optimality given above: the need for the planner to identify all possible alternative courses of action. Since it would be difficult, if not impossible, to determine whether the Indian educational planners had accomplished this task, it will be assumed that the only alternatives that need to be considered in the formulation of India's quantitative educational requirements involve the numbers of persons completing the three principal levels of the general (academic) educational system—primary, secondary, and university—and the order of priority according to which this education is to be provided.[8,9] It will further be assumed that such schooling is to be offered on a full-time basis to persons who have not yet entered adult occupations. The alternatives of allocating resources between the educational sector and other sectors, and within the educational sector between possible quantitative and qualitative objectives, will not be considered.

Another set of assumptions is concerned with the second criterion for optimality: full knowledge of the consequences of the various alternative courses of action. Although education may have many consequences for a society—direct and indirect—the only outcomes that will be considered in assessing the optimality of India's educational plans are those which were obviously considered by the educational planners: the benefits attributable to the relationship between education and national development, and the relative costs of providing different amounts of schooling.

[8] In view of the emphasis that is often given to the role of technical education in national development, it may be wondered why a limitation to general education should be adopted. First, it seems open to question whether vocationally oriented education is more important than general schooling. The latter appears to be at least as significant, since it provides the foundation for all other types of education and is often, in fact, the only kind of schooling that many members of underdeveloped societies are able to receive. Second, from the point of view of comparative research on the process of educational planning, a focus on the general educational system should have considerable interest, because requirements for general education are probably subject to more international regularities than vocational schooling, which may reflect to a greater extent the particular needs of each society.

[9] In establishing an order of priority, the problem is that of allocating resources in such a manner that maximum marginal benefits are obtained. See Charles J. Hitch and Roland N. McKean (1960, pp. 122–123).

Particularly intractable is the problem of evaluating the consequences of achieving various educational goals—the third criterion for an optimal formulation. The entire society would, presumably, have to pass judgment on the benefits and costs of any proposed educational objective. But how is this to be accomplished? Can a valid judgment be reached through existing governmental institutions, or is this procedure inadequate, considering the fact that the children who would be the recipients of the education provided or not provided would not take part in making the decision? This is only one of the issues involved in the problem of social choice, a considerable literature regarding which exists in the fields of welfare economics and political science.[10] In the present study it will be assumed that some indication of the desirability of particular priorities for educational development can be obtained from a consideration of India's experience with its educational system and from an examination of the body of informed Indian educational opinion. Additional support for the conclusions reached will be provided through the use of a hypothesis that describes the stages of development through which an educational system would be expected to pass if the most efficient use of the available resources were being made.

Through the use of the above limitations, it is believed that the important topic of the optimality of India's educational plans can be examined in this study on a rigorous and defensible basis. Nevertheless, it must be emphasized that the assessments of optimality presented and the conclusions drawn from them necessarily have only a qualified validity.

Organization of the Study

In Chapter II, a general description of the major features of the Indian educational system is provided. Chapter III is devoted to a consideration of India's quantitative educational requirements. The resulting interpretation is applied, in Chapter IV, to an assessment of the quantitative goals of the five major national educational plans that were in effect or were prepared during the period 1947–1961. In Chapter V, India's educational development during 1950–1961 is analyzed, utilizing various statistical measures to relate the actual growth achieved to the priorities envisioned in the educational plans. Finally, in Chapter VI, the conclusions obtained in this investigation are summarized and their implications briefly discussed.

---

[10] See, for example, the work of Kenneth J. Arrow (1951), Anthony Downs (1957), and James M. Buchanan and Gordon Tullock (1962).

II

Structure of the Indian
Educational System

Before attempting to discuss educational planning in India, it is necessary to have some understanding of the organization and control of the country's school system. As this study is concerned primarily with the quantitative development of the three major levels of the general (academic) educational system, it is essential for the interpretation of statistical data to know what types of schools comprise these levels, how many grades (years of study) are entailed, and the relationships among the educational levels. Also, since an educational plan, to be effective, must be acceptable to if not actually formulated by the persons responsible for establishing educational policies and exerting direction over the schools, it is important to know where this authority resides. This chapter will present, therefore, a brief description of the basic features in the structure of the Indian educational system.

Origins of the Present Pattern

The establishment in India of a modern educational system—that is, a system whose structure includes the university as a characteristic type of educational institution—is an outcome of the period of British rule.[1] Although the British through the East India Company had set up their first trading posts in India at the beginning of the seventeenth century, significant territorial acquisition did not take place until after the middle of the eighteenth century. The responsibility of government soon brought with it a concern for education. Charles Grant, an influential director of the East India Company with strong evangelical sentiments, was one of the earliest advocates of Western schooling for India. He saw education as a means of bringing Indians into closer association with their British rulers, spreading the benefits of Western civilization, and most important, facilitating the acceptance of the

---

[1] See below, pp. 17–18, for a discussion of the importance of the university in defining a modern school system.

9

Christian religion.[2] The efforts of Grant and others were eventually successful in persuading Parliament to authorize in the East India Act of 1813 an expenditure of £10,000 annually for the "revival and improvement of literature, and the encouragement of the learned natives of India, and for the introduction and promotion of a knowledge of the sciences among the inhabitants of the British territories in India." [3]

The British authorities in India, however, were not in agreement as to how the new educational policy should be applied. Three contrasting schools of thought may be identified. Two of them, known as the Orientalists and the Anglicists, would have given priority to the development of higher educational institutions and the training of an elite. But the Orientalists wanted to preserve as far as possible the traditional literary languages of India—Sanskrit, Persian, and Arabic— while the Anglicists insisted upon English as the medium of instruction. The third group was more interested in educating the mass of the population and thus emphasized the use of the vernacular languages.[4]

The conflict was eventually resolved in the Anglicists' favor. Asked to rule on a dispute between the Orientalists and the Anglicists on the General Committee of Public Instruction in Bengal, Thomas Macaulay prepared his famous Educational Minute of 1835, in which he vigorously espoused the cause of English education. Macaulay's views were endorsed by the Governor-General, Lord William Bentinck, who issued an Order in Council which declared

> . . . that the great object of the British Government ought to be the promotion of European literature and science among the natives of India; and that all the funds appropriated for the purposes of education would be best employed on English education alone.[5]

By the middle of the century, English schooling had made such progress that the need for a more comprehensive and systematic educational policy had become evident. This need was met by the Educational Despatch of 1854, which among several recommendations called for the creation of the first universities in India.[6] Accord-

---

[2] See Bruce T. McCully (1940, pp. 11–14).

[3] Quoted in McCully (1940, p. 18). For a detailed account of Grant's activities in support of Western schooling, see Elmer H. Cutts (1953).

[4] See Syed Nurullah and J. P. Naik (1943, pp. 68–88).

[5] Quoted in McCully (1940, pp. 69–70).

[6] The Despatch also stressed the role of the vernacular languages in the educational system, thus modifying the predominant position that had been given to English in Bentinck's earlier decision: "It is neither our aim nor desire to substitute the English language for the vernacular dialects of the country. We have

ingly, in 1857, universities were set up in Calcutta, Bombay, and Madras. This step—providing the essential institution—may be considered to mark the establishment of a modern educational system in the country.

The Educational Despatch of 1854 also helped to establish the principle of decentralized provincial control of education. The Despatch stipulated that departments of public instruction with the responsibility of inspecting government-supported schools and colleges were to be formed in each province.[7] To be sure, as long as India remained under British jurisdiction, some degree of central influence over educational policy was unavoidable. But this authority was reduced to a minimum when the Government of India Act of 1919 was implemented, giving control of education to Indian ministers of education responsible to representative provincial legislatures. The principle of decentralized provincial control over education was subsequently confirmed in the Government of India Act of 1935, which served as the country's basic legal framework until after its second year of independence.

Control of the Educational System

India received its independence on August 15, 1947. The Constitution, which was formally adopted on November 26, 1949, and came into force on January 26, 1950, prescribes the allocation of responsibility for education under the country's federal system of government. The Seventh Schedule of this document contains three lists in which the powers of the central government (List I), those of the states (List II), and those that are to be shared concurrently (List III) are enumerated. According to entry 11 in List II, the states have the authority to make laws regarding "education including universities"—a comprehensive statement of responsibility that gives the state governments virtually complete control over the educational facilities within their borders.

In 1961 the Union of India comprised fifteen states, all of equal status, and several small centrally administered areas and Union territories; the total population of the country was 439 million. With the exception of the state of Jammu and Kashmir, all of the Indian states

---

always been most sensible of the importance of the use of the languages which alone are understood by the great mass of the population. . . . We look, therefore, to the English language and to the vernacular languages of India together as the media for the diffusion of European knowledge, and it is our desire to see them cultivated together." Quoted in Nurullah and Naik (1943, pp. 161–162).

[7] See Nurullah and Naik (1943, pp. 162–163).

had populations greater than 10 million (Table 1). The largest state, Uttar Pradesh, had a population exceeding that of every country of the world except China, the U.S.S.R., the U.S.A., Indonesia, Pakistan, Japan, and, of course, India. The Union territories and centrally administered areas had less than 2 per cent of India's total population (Delhi, the largest Union territory, had a population of approximately two and one-half million). In 1963 a sixteenth state, Nagaland, was created from a previously centrally administered area; its population is about 400,000. A seventeenth state was formed in 1966, with the separation of Haryana from Punjab.

TABLE 1
Populations of the States of India, 1961

State	Total Population
Andhra Pradesh	35,980,000
Assam	11,870,000
Bihar	46,460,000
Gujarat	20,630,000
Jammu and Kashmir	3,560,000
Kerala	16,900,000
Madhya Pradesh	32,370,000
Madras	33,690,000
Maharashtra	39,550,000
Mysore	23,590,000
Orissa	17,550,000
Punjab	20,310,000
Rajasthan	20,160,000
Uttar Pradesh	73,750,000
West Bengal	34,930,000

The only limitation on the educational authority of the states is that which is imposed by the grant of certain other rights regarding educational matters to the central government by Lists I and III of the Constitution, or to the people in Part III (Fundamental Rights). Of these, three of the rights accorded the federal government are relevant to planning the quantitative development of the general educational system.[8] Most important for educational planning is entry 20 in List III, which authorizes the central and state governments to share the

[8] Some of the other limitations on state authority which are educationally significant in other respects include the right of religious and linguistic minorities to administer their own schools (Part III, Articles 29 and 30) and the right of the Union government to legislate concurrently with the states in regard to the "vocational and technical training of labour" (List III, entry 25).

responsibility for economic and social planning. As the result of the authority granted by entry 63 in List I, the Union government is responsible for certain universities and other institutions "declared by Parliament by law to be an institution of national importance"; but since the number of universities affected is small, this provision has relatively little effect upon the planning of the educational system as a whole. Entry 66 of the same list, which gives the federal government responsibility for the "coordination and determination of standards in institutions of higher education or research and scientific and technical institutions," is much more significant for the central control of higher education. The Union government has already used this right to justify the establishment of the University Grants Commission.[9] Depending on the interpretation given by the courts, the government may in the future succeed in developing an effective means of controlling university enrollments based on its authority to coordinate and determine standards for higher education.

Each of the states and the Union are governed by a legislature with a responsible council of ministers as its executive instrument. Under this parliamentary system, the government official with the primary responsibility for the development of educational policy and its execution is the minister who holds the education portfolio.[10] At the state level, the minister of education discharges his executive responsibilities through one or more directorates of education, headed by an official usually termed "the director of education" or "the director of public instruction." The principal functions of the director of education include the inspection of schools, the development of rules and regulations, the operation of certain educational institutions on behalf of the state, the collection of educational statistics, and the provision of technical advice in educational matters to the schools and the minister of education. In addition to the directorate of education, every state except West Bengal has a secretariat of education headed by an education secretary. This official works closely with the minister of education in the formulation of policy and for most purposes acts as the superior officer of the director of education.

For a discussion of several applications that have already been made of Articles 29 and 30, see M. V. Pylee (1960, pp. 262–272). Although these provisions have been important in preventing discriminatory educational practices, they cannot be used to prohibit the state from enforcing educational standards and presumably would not affect the right of the state to control educational enrollments if the purpose of this action were non-discriminatory.

[9] See below, p. 16.

[10] The education minister's responsibility is often less than complete, since certain types of education (such as technical and vocational training) may be allocated to another portfolio.

> Thus the proposals and policies submitted by the director of education [to the minister] are studied critically by the subordinate officers of the secretariat and as a result may be . . . presented in a form which may be quite different from what was originally conceived by the director.[11]

Other agencies may also participate in the process of educational decision-making at the state level, as a consequence of the delegation of state authority. A university, for example, is a semi-autonomous body, although it owes its existence to a legislative act. In most states, universities possess varying degrees of authority over the conduct of secondary schools, usually in connection with the administration of the high school–leaving examination, but sometimes extending to other areas as well. Advisory boards and councils may also be established to assist in the formulation of educational policy. Finally, local governmental authorities (district and municipal boards) and private agencies may be permitted to manage educational institutions. As shown in Table 2, only about a quarter of the educational institutions

TABLE 2
Management of Educational Institutions by
Different Agencies, 1958

| Management | Percentage of Total Number of Institutions Managed | | | |
	Primary Level	Middle Level	High School Level	University Level [a]
Government [b]	26.1	25.2	19.0	23.6
District boards	46.7	37.4	7.3	0.3 [c]
Municipal boards	3.0	3.1	2.8	0.0 [c]
Private bodies	24.2	34.3	70.9	76.0

[a] Arts and science colleges only.
[b] Includes state and central governments.
[c] Municipal boards included with figure for district boards.

at each of the major educational levels is actually managed by the state or central governments.[12] On the other hand, about two-thirds of the total educational expenditure comes from the state and central governments, with only a relatively small proportion (16.2 per cent) from district boards, municipal boards, and endowments (Table 3).

[11] See S. N. Mukerji (1962, p. 80).
[12] For a discussion of the types of educational institutions indicated in this and following tables, see below, pp. 18–30.

TABLE 3

Proportion of Total Educational Expenditure from Different Sources, 1958

Source of Funds	Percentage of Expenditure
Central government	7.3
State governments	58.3
District boards	4.0
Municipal boards	3.1
Fees	18.2
Endowments and other sources	9.1

The predominance of governmental support over that obtained from other sources applies to all levels except the university (Table 4), although student fees are also very important at the high school level.

TABLE 4

Proportion of Direct Expenditure on Institutions in Various Educational Levels from Different Sources, 1958 [a]

Source of Funds	Percentage of Expenditure on Each Educational Level			
	Primary	Middle	High School	University [b]
Central government	1.6	1.1	1.0	1.6
State governments	76.8	71.2	43.4	33.3
District boards	8.7	6.1	2.8	0.0
Municipal boards	7.4	2.7	1.7	0.1
Fees	2.6	12.2	41.5	53.0
Endowments and other sources	2.8	6.7	9.6	12.0

[a] Direct expenditures refer to those costs that can be specifically allocated to the various educational levels.

[b] Arts and science colleges only.

The federal government exercises most of its responsibilities for education through the Union Ministry of Education. In addition to its specific constitutional responsibilities, the Ministry performs a broad leadership function for Indian education, which is accomplished in three principal ways. One of the methods which the Ministry uses is that of coordination: meetings with state representatives are arranged, for example, in the expectation that useful ideas will emerge and gain wide acceptance. Another technique is that of providing financial assistance to the states to secure their cooperation in introducing changes designed to improve the quality of Indian education. The third device is that of undertaking activities which benefit all of the states, such as the collection of educational statistics and the sponsorship of educational research.

The Government of India has also established a number of advisory bodies to assist it in carrying out its educational responsibilities. Among these, the Central Advisory Board of Education and the University Grants Commission have an especially important role in determining national educational policy. Initially established in 1920, the Central Advisory Board of Education (CABE) is the oldest advisory body at the Union level and the one with the broadest scope for its deliberations. The CABE has the authority "to advise on any educational question which may be referred to it by the Government of India or by any local Government" and, on its own initiative, "to call for information and advice regarding educational developments of special interest or value to India; to examine this information and circulate it with recommendations to the Government of India and to local Governments." [13] Since the Union Minister of Education is chairman of the CABE and the education ministers of the states are all members, the decisions taken at its annual meetings—although not binding on either the federal or state governments—would represent the opinion of the nation's principal educational officials.

The University Grants Commission, patterned after the British University Grants Committee, was set up as an advisory committee in 1945, reconstituted in 1953, and then given a statutory basis in 1956. Its purpose, as stated in the University Grants Commission Act, is "to make provision for the coordination and determination of standards in Universities," a reference to the authority accorded the Union government by the Constitution. One of its principal functions is to "inquire into the financial needs of Universities" and to distribute out of its funds grants "for the maintenance and development of such Universities." The Commission is also authorized to "advise the Central Government or any State Government on the allocation of any grants to Universities." [14] To the extent that it is provided with funds to disburse to the universities and its advice on spending other funds is accepted, the University Grants Commission is clearly in a powerful position to influence the decisions that are taken in the Indian universities.

---

[13] India, *Resolution* No. F. 122–3/35-E (August 8, 1935), as amended up to June 12, 1962.
[14] India, *University Grants Commission Act* (1956).

Levels of Education: The Problem of Terminology

The schools comprising the educational systems of most countries of the world may be divided into three sequential levels: primary, secondary, and university. This regularity may be attributed to the nearly universal occurrence of the university as a type of educational institution. In serving to demarcate the highest level of a school system, the university also fixes the length of the university-preparatory course (about twelve years in most countries). But since no society has yet deemed it appropriate to provide universal education at the university level, in school systems with unrestricted initial access to education a separation of students according to different curriculums or even different educational institutions takes place somewhere during the period of university-preparatory schooling. This point at which an effective bifurcation into university-preparatory and non-university-preparatory courses takes place marks the division between the primary and secondary levels.[15]

A few decades ago students in the educational systems of many countries began their initial studies in two different types of schools. One type was designed to prepare its students for university entrance; the other was essentially terminal in nature and provided only the "elements" of knowledge. In this kind of school system—generally referred to as a two-track system—the vertical divisions, rather than the horizontal, are of principal importance. With a widespread acceptance of the concept of mass education, however, the two-track educational system has largely given way to a system with a single track for the initial period of schooling. In a single-track system, all students begin their studies in the same type of school and follow an identical curriculum (the primary level), thus theoretically having an equivalent opportunity of entering the university-preparatory course at the secondary level.[16]

An educational system in which a university or equivalent institu-

[15] The problem of classifying the structure of educational systems is also considered (though not necessarily in a similar way) in UNESCO, *World Survey of Education* (1955); UNESCO, *World Survey of Education*, Vol. III: *Secondary Education* (1961); Frank Bowles (1963); and Michel Debeauvais (1966).

[16] Certain educational systems may seem to have differentiated curriculums at the primary level (as a consequence, for example, of curriculum differences between public and private schools or urban and rural schools), but these variations are usually not important enough in themselves effectively to bar students attending one type of school from access to the university. If curriculum differences at the primary level did result in such a predetermination of further educational opportunity, then the school system could not be designated a single-track system.

tion is present will be designated a "modern" school system. The term "modern" is used only for the purpose of providing a general label by which educational systems that prepare students for the university can be differentiated from educational systems that are not so oriented, such as the "bush schools" of Africa. It is recognized that considerable differences may exist within this category, and that some of the educational systems may be more "modern" in a functional sense than others.

The expression "higher education" is frequently encountered in educational terminology and consequently also needs to be defined. In a modern school system this level would consist of all of the educational institutions which serve approximately the same age group as the university and require approximately the same number of years of preparatory schooling (though not necessarily of the same type). However, in view of the limitation of this study to general education, attention will necessarily be focused on the university rather than other types of higher educational institutions.

The Levels of the Indian Educational System

In the Indian school system, it is difficult to determine what constitutes primary and secondary education. The main reason for this problem is not the presence of a two-track educational system but the absence of any meaningful form of allocation of students during the approximately eleven years of school (which thus far has been considerably less than universal) that precedes the university level. As a consequence, almost all of the education imparted during this period is university preparatory, and thus there is no functional basis on which to distinguish the primary and secondary levels. However, the desire of educational officials to provide at least a minimum amount of schooling to all students has led them to regard the four or five years required to produce permanent literacy as the duration of primary education. But it has also been recognized that ideally all children should receive seven or eight years of education to prepare them for effective citizenship; accordingly, this period of schooling has also been called primary education. (The term "elementary education" has been used by Indian educators interchangeably with "primary education" in reference to both the minimum and ideal periods of universal schooling, but this does not help to clarify the issue.) To further complicate the terminology, a third level known as "middle school" is often distinguished by Indian educators. This level comprises about three years of schooling and is intermediate between the first four or five years of schooling and the final segment, or "high school" level of the university-preparatory course, which comprises approximately three years. Thus, in carrying out this investigation, it will frequently be necessary to deal with the three levels of primary school, middle school, and high school, rather than simply "primary" and "secondary" levels. Where required, however, primary education will be considered to comprise the initial four or five years of schooling, and the combination of middle school and high school will be taken as equivalent to the secondary level.

Another problem concerns the delimitation of the university level itself. Prior to independence, the instruction provided by the universities was generally of four years' duration and consisted of two courses: a two-year intermediate college course and a two-year university course leading to the first (bachelor's) degree in arts and science. As a result of the reforms discussed below, the first-degree course now usually comprises three years of study and the old intermediate course has been largely eliminated. But the first year of the intermediate course has not been completely replaced by an extension of the university-preparatory course; the universities, therefore, have offered a pre-university course of one year's duration for students who have completed only the standard secondary school program. Thus, the length of education provided by the universities for the majority of students has remained four years, but consisting of a "1 + 3" rather than a "2 + 2" pattern. For the purposes of the present study, the university level will be considered to consist of the courses for the first and higher university degrees, the pre-university course, and the intermediate course where it is offered.[17]

In interpreting the statistics, it is important to note the distinction between data referring to educational *institutions* and to educational *levels*. Some of the available data are compiled with respect to institutions such as primary schools, high schools, or arts and sciences colleges, but it is possible that a high school, for example, may also provide classes at the middle level and even the primary level. The institutional statistics for India, however, do not ordinarily reflect this fact; a high school would be returned only as a high school (rather than as two or three different types of institutions), regardless of the actual grades involved.[18] In the present investigation, statistics for levels of instruction will be utilized where possible in place of data according to educational institutions.

Because of differences among the educational structures of the

[17] For a definition of general education at the university level, see below, p. 30.
[18] This problem is also discussed in UNESCO, *Manual of Educational Statistics* (1961, pp. 140–141).

states, India does not have a uniform national pattern of schooling. For certain purposes, of course, by minimizing differences and emphasizing similarities, it is possible to discuss an Indian system of education. But for any careful analysis, it is vital to distinguish among the various state school systems. Before examining the organization of education in the states, however, it will be useful to consider the efforts that have been made to create a system of schools that is more uniform.

Attempts to Establish a National Educational Pattern

The lack of a suitable national pattern for Indian education was severely criticized in the country's first educational plan, the Central Advisory Board of Education (CABE) Plan of 1944. "The present system," the CABE contended, "does not provide the foundations on which an effective structure could be erected; in fact much of the present rambling edifice will have to be scrapped in order that something better may be substituted." [19] At the primary level, the CABE recommended the establishment of a unitary school of five grades for the age group 6–10.[20] This school, to be known as the "junior basic school," would provide a modified form of the "basic education" originally advocated by Mahatma Gandhi.[21] After completion of the primary level, 20 percent of the pupils would be selected for admission to a high school, while the remaining 80 percent would finish their education in senior basic schools of three years' duration. The high school level would be divided into two sequential programs, both three years in length. Thus the total time required for a student to gain university entrance would be eleven years. The CABE also advocated a significant alteration in the pattern of the university program for the first degree, which at the time the plan was prepared involved four years of study subdivided into two courses of two years each (the intermediate college course and the degree course), by calling for the abolition of the intermediate college and the institution of a three-year first-degree program.[22]

Since the attainment of Indian independence, two important committees have dealt with the problems of university and secondary

---

[19] India, Bureau of Education, *Post-War Educational Development in India,* A Report by the Central Advisory Board of Education, January, 1944 (5th ed.; Delhi: Manager of Publications, 1947), p. 2.

[20] In conformity with standard demographic practice, age groups referred to in this investigation will be given in inclusive years.

[21] See below, pp. 26–28.

[22] India, Bureau of Education, *Post-War Educational Development in India,* pp. 6–21, 29.

education respectively. These have been the University Education Commission, which concluded its work in 1949, and the Secondary Education Commission, whose report was presented in 1953. The University Education Commission agreed with the CABE in suggesting that university education for the first degree should be modified to require three years of study instead of two and that the intermediate course of two years be eliminated. The Commission, however, recommended that university-preparatory schooling comprise twelve years, in contrast to the eleven-year program which the CABE had considered adequate.[23] The Secondary Education Commission also endorsed the proposal for transforming the program for the first degree at the university level into a three-year course, but it recommended either eleven or twelve years as the appropriate length of university-preparatory schooling. The pattern which it suggested involved a primary school of four or five years, to be followed by a middle level of three years and a higher secondary course of four years. The establishment of the higher secondary course (which would generally require extending the existing high school course by one year) would compensate for the proposed reduction in the length of education at the university level.[24]

In their consideration of the report of the Secondary Education Commission, both the CABE and the Union Ministry of Education sought to reduce the variability in the proposed length of the university-preparatory course. The last grade of the secondary level, the CABE suggested, should be designated the eleventh and could be reached "*after* schooling of not less than ten years, the actual duration of the school system in the various States to be determined by the State Governments concerned." [25] The CABE's action was followed by a statement from the Union Ministry of Education in which the outlines of the "future pattern of education" were given, expressing the consensus which appeared to have "at last been reached." The Ministry envisioned an educational system of three levels. The first level would consist of "eight years of integrated Elementary (Basic) education" for the age group 6–13; the second would comprise "three years of Secondary education" for the age group 14–16; the third would entail "three years of University education after the Higher Secondary school, leading to the first Degree." The Ministry felt that stipulation of the age for the completion of secondary school-

[23] India, Ministry of Education, *The Report of the University Education Commission (December 1948–August 1949)* (1st reprint ed.; Delhi: Manager of Publications, 1963), p. 134.

[24] India, Ministry of Education, *Report of the Secondary Education Commission* (4th reprint ed.; Delhi: Manager of Publications, 1958), p. 230.

[25] Quoted in India, Ministry of Education, *A Plan for Secondary Education* (Delhi: Manager of Publications, 1955), pp. 1–2.

ing (seventeen-plus) would insure that a uniform standard of achievement prevailed throughout the country, even if some states attempted to increase the length of the university-preparatory course by commencing primary education at an earlier age than six.[26]

As a result of generous financial assistance from the University Grants Commission, by 1961 the three-year pattern for the first degree course had been widely accepted, with the state of Uttar Pradesh and Bombay University representing the only holdouts.[27] However, as indicated above, the corollary reform of introducing the higher secondary course in place of the high school course has not met with the same success, thus requiring a pre-university course of one year to be given at the university level.[28]

The effort to achieve a satisfactory national pattern of education is still continuing. Recently the Government of India, in a resolution dated July 14, 1964, announced the appointment of an Education Commission to survey the entire educational system and to advise the government on the national pattern of education. The Commission was headed by D. S. Kothari, Chairman of the University Grants Commission, and it submitted its report on June 29, 1966. In this report, the Education Commission placed major emphasis on improving the quality of Indian education. Structural change by itself, the Commission contended, would not be sufficient. Nevertheless, the Commission believed that certain structural changes should be introduced. Among the most significant changes advocated by the Commission are the lengthening of the university-preparatory course to twelve years and the abandonment of the attempt to convert all high schools to higher secondary schools (the major reform advocated in the earlier report of the Secondary Education Commission). The educational structure recommended by the Education Commission would consist, therefore, of the following pattern for the university-preparatory course: a primary course of seven or eight years; a lower secondary course of three or two years, the total length of both courses to comprise ten years; and a higher secondary course of two years, which would constitute "an independent, self-contained unit like the Sixth Form in England." Only about one-fourth of the secondary schools would provide the higher secondary course.[29] Whether these recommendations will be generally adopted remains to be seen.

[26] *Ibid.*, pp. i, 2–8. See also Humayun Kabir (1959, pp. 64–69).

[27] India, Ministry of Education, *Report of the Committee on Emotional Integration* (Delhi: Manager of Publications, 1962), p. 217.

[28] In Kerala the pre-university course is two years.

[29] India, Ministry of Education, *Report of the Education Commission: 1964–66* (Delhi: Manager of Publications, 1966), pp. 23–45.

Structure of Education in the States

The various state patterns of primary and secondary education prevailing in 1961 are shown in Table 5. As this table reveals, the

TABLE 5

States, Patterns of Primary and Secondary Schooling, 1961

State	Course	Grades [a]	Duration (Years)
Andhra Pradesh	Primary	I–V	5
	Middle	VI–VIII	3
	High school	IX–XI	3
	Higher secondary	IX–XII	4
Assam	Primary	I–V	5
	Middle	VI–VIII	3
	High school	IX–XII	4
	Higher secondary	IX–XIII	5
Bihar	Primary	I–V	5
	Middle	VI–VII [b]	2 [b]
	High school	VIII–XI [c]	4
	Higher secondary	VIII–XII	5
Gujarat:			
(1) Gujarat region	Primary	I–IV	4
	Middle	V–VII	3
	High school	VIII–XI	4
(2) Saurashtra region	Primary	I–IV	4
	Middle	V–VIII	4
	High school	IX–XI	3
(3) Kutch region	Primary	I–V	5
	Middle	VI–VIII	3
	High school	IX–XII	4
Jammu and Kashmir	Primary	I–V	5
	Middle	VI–VIII	3
	High school	IX–X	2
	Higher secondary	IX–XI	3
Kerala	Primary	I–IV	4
	Middle	V–VII	3
	High school	VIII–X	3

TABLE 5—*Continued*
States, Patterns of Primary and Secondary Schooling, 1961

State	Course	Grades [a]	Duration (Years)
Madhya Pradesh	Primary	I–V	5
	Middle	VI–VIII	3
	High school	IX–X	2
	Higher secondary	IX–XI	3
Madras	Primary	I–V	5
	Middle	VI–VIII	3
	High school	IX–XI	3
Maharashtra:			
(1) Former Bombay State	Primary	I–IV	4
	Middle	V–VII	3
	High school	VIII–XI	4
(2) Vidarbha region	Primary	I–IV	4
	Middle	V–VIII	4
	High school	IX–X	2
	Higher secondary	IX–XI	3
(3) Marathwada region	Primary	I–V	5
	Middle	VI–VIII	3
	High school	IX–XI	3
	Higher secondary	IX–XII	4
Mysore:			
(1) Former Mysore State	Primary	I–IV, I–V	4/5
	Middle	V–VIII, VI–VIII [d]	4/3 [d]
	High school	IX–XI	3
(2) Former Bombay State	Primary	I–IV	4
	Middle	V–VII	3
	High school	VIII–XI	4
(3) Former Madras State and Coorg region	Primary	I–V	5
	Middle	VI–VIII	3
	High school	IX–XI	3
(4) Former Hyderabad State	Primary	I–V	5
	Middle	VI–VIII	3
	High school	IX–XI	3
	Higher secondary	IX–XII	4
Orissa	Primary	I–V	5
	Middle	VI–VII [e]	2 [e]
	High school	VIII–XI [f]	4
	Higher secondary	VIII–XII	5

TABLE 5—Continued

States, Patterns of Primary and Secondary Schooling, 1961

State	Course	Grades [a]	Duration (Years)
Punjab	Primary	I–V	5
	Middle	VI–VIII	3
	High school	IX–X	2
	Higher secondary	IX–XI	3
Rajasthan	Primary	I–V	5
	Middle	VI–VIII	3
	High school	IX–X	2
	Higher secondary	IX–XI	3
Uttar Pradesh	Primary	I–V	5
	Middle	VI–VIII	3
	High school	IX–X	2
West Bengal	Primary	I–IV [g]	4 [g]
	Middle	V–VIII [h]	4 [h]
	High school	IX–X	2
	Higher secondary	IX–XI	3

[a] The designations of grades given do not always conform to those in use by the states. A state may, for example, actually refer to the first grade as "Infant Class," the second grade as "Class I," and so forth.

[b] Senior basic schools have grades VI–VIII, duration three years.

[c] Post-basic schools have grades IX–XII.

[d] Grades V–VIII in areas with four-year primary schools; grades VI–VIII in areas with five-year primary schools.

[e] Senior basic schools have grades VI–VIII, duration three years.

[f] Post-basic schools have grades IX–XII.

[g] Junior basic schools have grades I–V, duration five years.

[h] Senior basic schools have grades VI–VIII, duration three years.

total length of university-preparatory schooling (excluding basic education and the higher secondary course) was twelve years in one state (Assam), eleven years in seven states (Andhra Pradesh, Bihar, Gujarat,[30] Madras, Maharashtra,[31] Mysore, and Orissa) and ten years in the remaining seven states (Jammu and Kashmir, Kerala, Madhya Pradesh, Punjab, Rajasthan, Uttar Pradesh, and West Bengal). Higher secondary schools were present in all but four of the states (Gujarat, Kerala, Madras, and Uttar Pradesh), though their number was less than 21 percent of the total number of high schools and higher secondary schools in every state except Madhya Pradesh, Rajasthan, and

[30] In the Kutch region of Gujarat twelve years were required.

[31] In the Vidarbha region of Maharashtra ten years were required.

West Bengal (Table 6). There were also regional differences in the educational patterns of three states (Gujarat, Maharashtra, and Mysore) resulting from the reorganization and amalgamation of previously existing states and the maintenance of the original school structures of these areas.

TABLE 6
States, Numbers of High and Higher Secondary Schools, 1961

State	Combined Number of High and Higher Secondary Schools	Number of Higher Secondary Schools	Number of Higher Secondary Schools as Percent of Combined Number
Andhra Pradesh	1,192	140	11.7
Assam	631	45	7.1
Bihar	1,500	122	8.1
Gujarat	834	0	0.0
Jammu and Kashmir	262	24	9.2
Kerala	891	0	0.0
Madhya Pradesh	801	701	87.5
Madras	1,468	0	0.0
Maharashtra	2,468	95	3.8
Mysore	750	69	9.2
Orissa	400	7	1.8
Punjab	1,341	272	20.3
Rajasthan	542	308	56.8
Uttar Pradesh	954	0	0.0
West Bengal	1,825	743	40.7

Another source of structural differentiation in the state school systems has been the attempt to introduce "basic education." Basic schools comprise three levels—junior basic, senior basic, and post-basic—which are parallel to the primary, middle, and high school levels of the non-basic system.[32] The distinguishing feature of basic education, as propounded by Mahatma Gandhi, its originator, is the concept of *correlated craft teaching*. Gandhi explained his approach to the All-India National Educational Conference which convened to examine his scheme at Wardha in October, 1937: "I want the whole process of education to be imparted through some handicrafts or industry."[33] His idea was that a student, while learning a craft, could

[32] Instead of going to the universities, students who wish to continue their education after completing the post-basic level may attend a rural institute, the counterpart in the basic education system to the university.

[33] See T. S. Avinashilingam (1960, p. 57).

acquire the knowledge that was related to it, and through this method learn most, if not all, that was in the curriculum. Gandhi's proposal was considered and approved in 1938 by a committee appointed by the CABE; the report of this committee was adopted by the Board in the same year without alteration. In its report the committee noted that one of the main principles of basic education required that "all training should so far as possible be given through a profit-yielding vocation." [34]

While advocates of basic education have conceded that not all knowledge can be acquired by means of a craft, this aspect of the approach represents its central feature: without the emphasis on cor-related craft teaching, basic education would be little different from other educational concepts that involve activity methods of teaching. Basic education rests on the assumption that every child will learn more effectively if one teaching method (craft correlation) is followed, yet it seems obvious that some children may learn better through various other methods, depending on what is being taught.[35] The learning of a craft, therefore, would appear to entail a sacrifice in terms of inadequate learning of other subjects—either because the craft correlation method is inappropriate for teaching them or simply because the amount of time spent in acquiring proficiency in the tech-niques of the craft does not permit enough attention to be given elsewhere.

It is thus hardly surprising that the proportion of students en-rolled in basic schools is relatively small: in 1960, only 18 percent of the students enrolled in schools at the primary and middle levels —excluding those in Uttar Pradesh—were in basic institutions.[36] The numbers of basic schools in the states are shown in Table 7. While most of the so-called basic schools are probably basic in name only— as clearly seems to be the case in Uttar Pradesh—their separate orga-

[34] India, Ministry of Education, *Reports of the Committees Appointed by the Central Advisory Board of Education in India (1938–43)* (Delhi: Manager of Pub-lications, 1958), p. 1.

[35] While it presumably should be within the province of the teacher to select the method of instruction that is most suitable for a given set of circumstances, in basic education the fundamental method is predetermined. Although this is not the place to analyze the deficiencies of the basic education concept, its principal shortcoming would seem to be that children generally lack interest in craft work. Activity methods of teaching depend upon an inherent interest in the particular activity that is employed and a transfer of this interest to the acquisition of the knowledge associated with the activity.

[36] Calculated from statistics contained in India, Ministry of Education, *Educa-tion in the States: 1959–60* (Delhi: Manager of Publications, 1962). Very few post-basic schools exist. Uttar Pradesh is omitted from the calculation because *all* primary and middle schools are classified as basic, a most doubtful attainment (see Table 7).

TABLE 7

States, Numbers of Basic and Non-Basic Schools, 1960

				School Type		
					High/	
		Junior		Senior	Higher	Post-
State	Primary	Basic	Middle	Basic	Secondary	Basic
Andhra Pradesh	30,084	2,472	509	308	1,080	2
Assam	12,627	2,388	1,418	211	484	0
Bihar	32,903	2,698	3,372	768	1,428	21
Gujarat [a]	10,308	1,724	3,299	3,181	1,099	0
Jammu and Kashmir	2,754	0	457	0	192	0
Kerala	6,392	440	1,800	123	870	2
Madhya Pradesh	25,110	2,369	1,857	297	634	0
Madras	20,470	3,046	2,301	546	1,105	3
Maharashtra [a]	23,905	1,513	6,716	2,730	2,198	0
Mysore	21,704	1,939	886	1,297	664	0
Orissa	20,023	361	1,088	23	405	2
Punjab	11,922	777	1,289	73	1,339	4
Rajasthan	11,240	1,801	1,194	62	458	0
Uttar Pradesh	0	38,049	0	4,184	954 [a]	0
West Bengal	25,912	1,297	2,069	133	1,847	0

[a] Data for 1961.

nization within the state school systems has produced structural variations in the educational patterns of Bihar, Orissa, and West Bengal (Table 5). If significant curricular differences are also associated with basic schools (such as a failure to teach English, which is the language of instruction in many university programs), a two-track educational system would result, but it has not been possible to ascertain the extent to which this pattern exists, if at all.

Yet another factor responsible for structural differentiation is the presence of multi-purpose schools at the secondary level. As a means of alleviating the apparent imbalance between general and vocational education, the Secondary Education Commission had advocated the provision of multi-purpose (comprehensive) secondary schools. "Our secondary schools," the Commission explained, "should no longer be 'single-track' institutions but should offer a diversity of educational programmes calculated to meet varying aptitudes, interests and talents." [37] In 1962, a total of 1,389 multi-purpose high schools

[37] India, Ministry of Education, *Report of the Secondary Education Commission* (Delhi: Manager of Publications, 1958, p. 36).

were reported to have been established, compared to about 17,000 high and higher secondary schools.[38] Since students enrolled in the vocational programs of multi-purpose schools are usually eligible for admission to the arts and science course at the university level, these schools will, for the purposes of the present study, be regarded as essentially equivalent to high and higher secondary schools.[39]

The Pattern of University Education

Education at the university level in India is characterized by a unique pattern of universities and affiliated colleges, which was introduced with the establishment of the first universities in 1857. Modeled after the University of London, the Indian universities were initially set up to prescribe courses of study in the colleges affiliated to them, to examine candidates prepared in these colleges, and to grant degrees. The affiliating system allowed colleges to be opened in remote places and, while permitting considerable diversity in religious and social life, maintained standards through the requirement of common examinations.[40]

In 1961, India had a total of forty-six universities, thirty-two of which were of the affiliating type. Nearly all of the affiliating universities by then also provided instruction in their own teaching departments or in constituent colleges. In the non-affiliating universities, instruction was generally confined to university teaching departments and constituent or associated colleges located within a limited geographical area.[41] There were 1,544 affiliated, associated, or constituent colleges in 1961, which may be classified in three main instructional categories: arts and science colleges, which offer general education; professional colleges, such as those providing instruction in the fields of commerce, medicine, engineering, and education; and colleges for special education, which include the fields of oriental studies and fine

[38] India, Ministry of Education, *Provisional Educational Statistics (as on 31st March, 1962)* (New Delhi: Ministry of Education, 1962).

[39] In any case, with few exceptions, multi-purpose schools are not differentiated from other types of high schools in the available statistical data.

[40] *Commonwealth Universities Yearbook: 1963* (1963, pp. 459–463).

[41] India, Ministry of Education, *Directory of Institutions for Higher Education: 1961* (Delhi: Manager of Publications, 1961), pp. 3–10. Some instruction may also be given in institutes recognized by the universities. Although not statutory universities, several "institutions of national importance," as declared by Acts of Parliament, and institutions "deemed as universities under Section 3 of the University Grants Commission Act," are regarded as equivalent to universities in status. *Ibid.*, p. 124; K. G. Saiyidain and H. C. Gupta (1962, pp. 12–13).

arts.[42] A total of 988 colleges providing the intermediate course were affiliated to state boards of education in 1961 (most of them in Uttar Pradesh); some of these colleges were also affiliated to universities for degree courses and are thus included in the total of 1,544 given above.[43]

The complicated structure of university-level education in India makes it essential to specify the types of statistical data that will be used in this study. Since the primary concern of the investigation is with general education, most of the data presented will relate to arts and science programs at the university level. These programs will be referred to as "the general education course" or "education in the arts and science faculties." For certain purposes, commerce education will also be included in this category, because this type of training is functionally very similar to arts and science education, and is so regarded in current educational planning. In some instances where data for the university *level* are not available, *institutional* statistics for arts and science (or arts, science, and commerce) colleges will be utilized, but since these data omit university teaching departments, for example, and may include enrollments in non-university-level courses, they are subject to the limitations of institutional data indicated above.[44] Occasionally statistics for education in all programs at the university level will be used for comparisons with the general education course.

Transition between Educational Levels

The final aspect of the structure of Indian education to be considered in this chapter is the transition between the levels of the school system. Various methods of controlling access to an educational level may be used, such as selective entrance examinations, fees, and a rigorous curriculum which induces failure and wastage. However, the concern here will not be primarily with the nature of the techniques, but with their effects.

[42] See India, Ministry of Education, *Directory of Institutions for Higher Education: 1961*, pp. 12–126. The threefold classification of colleges according to subjects taught is that used by the Union Ministry of Education in its annual statistical publication, *Education in India*. In another annual statistical publication, *Education in Universities in India*, the Ministry uses only two categories: general and professional education. The University Grants Commission in its recent statistical reports employs fundamentally the same two categories, with arts, science, and commerce colleges regarded as one type and professional colleges the other.

[43] India, Ministry of Education, *Directory of Institutions for Higher Education: 1961*, pp. 137–164.

[44] See p. 19.

If effective procedures for limiting initial access from one educational level to another are being employed, it would be expected that the transition rates between levels should be lower than the transition rates prevailing between other grades in the school system. But as Table 8 reveals, the apparent transition rate [45] from one grade

TABLE 8

India, Apparent Transition between Grades, Primary and Secondary Levels, 1960–1961

Grades	Enrollment of Lower Grade in 1960 (Thousands)	Enrollment of Higher Grade in 1961 (Thousands)	1961 Enrollment, as Percentage of 1960 Enrollment
Males			
I to II	8,342	5,040	60.4
II to III	4,827	4,020	83.3
III to IV	3,710	3,214	86.6
IV to V	3,001	2,585	86.1
V to VI	2,415	2,033	84.2
VI to VII	1,937	1,672	86.3
VII to VIII	1,482	1,365	92.1
VIII to IX	1,202	1,023	85.1
IX to X	930	860	92.5
Females			
I to II	4,350	2,462	56.6
II to III	2,320	1,849	79.7
III to IV	1,681	1,376	81.9
IV to V	1,247	1,020	81.8
V to VI	925	692	74.8
VI to VII	656	546	83.2
VII to VIII	444	391	88.1
VIII to IX	331	255	77.0
IX to X	217	187	86.2

in 1960 to the next consecutive grade in 1961 is nearly constant for the university-preparatory course except between grades I and II. Before valid conclusions can be reached, however, an analysis by the

[45] While it would be preferable for this analysis to have statistics on the numbers of graduates from the lower grade and new entrants into the higher grade, these data are unavailable. Hence the rate given, which is based on total enrollment statistics, must be referred to as an "apparent" transition rate. Such enrollment data serve to give an approximation of the numbers required.

relevant grades is necessary, because the first and terminal grades of the various educational levels are not the same in all states. But as shown in Tables 9 and 10, the apparent transition rates between the

TABLE 9
India, Apparent Transition between Primary and Middle Levels, 1961–1962

Sex	Enrollment in Last Grade of Primary Level, 1961	Enrollment in First Grade of Middle Level, 1962	1962 Enrollment, as Percentage of 1961 Enrollment
Male	2,842,450	2,390,938	84.1
Female	1,162,864	874,515	75.2

TABLE 10
India, Apparent Transition between Middle and High School Levels, 1961–1962

Sex	Enrollment in Last Grade of Middle Level, 1961	Enrollment in First Grade of High School Level, 1962	1962 Enrollment, as Percentage of 1961 Enrollment
Male	1,546,043	1,295,533	83.8
Female	481,669	378,154	78.5

primary and middle levels and between the middle and high school levels, respectively, are found to correspond very closely to the rates for all grades given in Table 8. Moreover, as shown in Tables 11 and 12, no state departs significantly from the averages for India as a whole.

The apparent transition rates from the high school to the university level are presented in Table 13. To the extent that these rates are valid, they indicate—since they are lower than the rates prevailing within the university-preparatory period of schooling—that some limitation of initial access to the university level is taking place. Table 14, which is based on the numbers of students who were eligible for university admission in 1960 by virtue of success in the high school–leaving examination or a comparable examination given by a university (these students are generally referred to as "matriculates"), suggests that failure to begin the first year of study at the university level rather than inability to complete the high school course is primarily responsible for the lower transition rate.

TABLE 11

States, Apparent Transition between Primary and Middle Levels, 1961–1962

State	Enrollment in Last Grade of Primary Level, 1961		Enrollment in First Grade of Middle Level, 1962		1962 Enrollment, as Percentage of 1961 Enrollment	
	Male	Female	Male	Female	Male	Female
Andhra Pradesh	190,691	94,959	147,561	48,125	77.4	50.7
Assam	71,205	35,228	62,981	26,809	88.5	76.1
Bihar	221,688	43,502	192,784	27,659	87.0	63.6
Gujarat	177,544	86,511	158,614	68,472	89.3	79.1
Jammu and Kashmir	21,777	5,578	20,690	6,211	95.0	111.3
Kerala	229,093	193,014	187,789	152,806	82.0	79.2
Madhya Pradesh	158,686	38,200	124,423	30,870	78.4	80.8
Madras	258,108	137,398	213,318	99,136	82.6	72.2
Maharashtra	365,080	172,721	316,728	130,159	86.8	75.4
Mysore	131,558	59,025	117,851	49,734	89.6	84.3
Orissa	55,662	9,871	45,650	7,109	82.0	72.0
Punjab	156,671	58,012	144,428	43,290	92.2	74.6
Rajasthan	91,829	18,798	91,879	14,787	100.1	78.7
Uttar Pradesh	356,687	80,988	314,191	57,408	88.1	70.9
West Bengal	238,373	101,026	197,483	82,847	82.8	82.0

TABLE 12

States, Apparent Transition between Middle and High School Levels, 1961–1962

State	Enrollment in Last Grade of Middle Level, 1961		Enrollment in First Grade of High School Level, 1962		1962 Enrollment, as Percentage of 1961 Enrollment	
	Male	Female	Male	Female	Male	Female
Andhra Pradesh	85,065	22,003	72,007	16,353	84.6	74.3
Assam	46,795	17,636	35,686	12,194	76.3	69.1
Bihar	157,925	19,153	144,291	11,798	91.4	61.6
Gujarat	93,007	37,689	80,016	27,685	86.0	73.5
Jammu and Kashmir	14,407	3,050	12,377	3,001	85.9	98.4
Kerala	150,107	112,485	132,415	99,326	88.2	88.3
Madhya Pradesh	70,765	12,132	52,230	10,726	73.8	88.4
Madras	125,121	52,579	96,922	35,893	77.5	68.3
Maharashtra	179,324	64,280	162,730	51,103	90.7	79.5
Mysore	68,857	23,650	57,986	18,478	84.2	78.1
Orissa	33,693	4,144	30,383	2,139	90.2	51.6
Punjab	94,202	23,241	79,514	18,896	84.4	81.3
Rajasthan	45,873	6,105	48,108	4,650	104.9	76.2
Uttar Pradesh	211,893	32,595	172,835	23,102	81.6	70.9
West Bengal	107,358	33,787	95,082	28,141	88.6	83.3

TABLE 13

India, Apparent Transition between High School and
University Levels, 1961–1962

Sex	Enrollment in Last Grade of High School Level, 1961	Enrollment in First Year of Pre-university/ Intermediate Course, 1962	1962 Enrollment, as Percentage of 1961 Enrollment
Male	622,658	285,802	45.9
Female	133,559	59,054	44.2

TABLE 14

India, Apparent Transition between High School and
University Levels, 1960–1961

Sex	Number of Matriculates, 1960	Enrollment in First Year of Pre-university/ Intermediate Course, 1961	1961 Enrollment, as Percentage of 1960 Matriculates
Male	429,234	226,481	52.8
Female	115,606	48,535	42.0

As a recent survey by Saiyidain and Gupta has demonstrated, however, this limitation of initial access is the consequence of only minimal efforts to control university admissions. Saiyidain and Gupta discovered that out of 156 arts and science colleges which replied to a question about enrollment quotas, 53 had no fixed ceilings on enrollment. Perhaps more significantly, only four of the colleges had enrollment ceilings which were set by the government. Of 159 arts and sciences colleges answering a question on their entrance requirements, 134 stated that they accepted students who had secured only the minimum passing scores in the high school–leaving exminations.[46]

Very few data are available from which the extent of wastage at the university level may be determined. An extremely tentative conclusion that the amount of wastage within the university level is equivalent to that within the university-preparatory course may be drawn from a study by Kamat and Deshmukh on wastage in one of the colleges of Poona University. Kamat and Deshmukh found that approximately 57 percent of the students beginning the arts course

[46] See K. G. Saiyidain and H. C. Gupta (1962, pp. 96–97).

and 64 percent beginning the science course in 1949–1951 eventually obtained their degrees.[47] These figures show a wastage over the four-year university course that is about the same as that which would exist during four years of the university-preparatory course, using the apparent transition rates shown in Table 8.

The preceding analysis thus indicates that the transition rates within the Indian educational system are relatively uniform. Although this does not mean that the school system is non-selective—because wastage is one way of effecting selection—it does imply that, in the absence of other methods of controlling access between educational levels [48] and as long as transition rates remain uniform, an increase of enrollment at a lower level will result in a corresponding expansion at higher levels. The importance of this fact will become evident later when the implementation of India's educational plans is examined.

[47] See A. R. Kamat and A. G. Deshmukh (1963).

[48] J. P. Naik (1965, Paper No. 3, pp. 30–31) has commented as follows on the failure to use fees to control access: "the people now demand 'free' education not only at the elementary stage [level] but also at the secondary and university stages. . . . The Congress [party] Manifesto issued at Bhubaneswar speaks of a programme of providing free education till the end of the secondary stage. The policy has already been adopted in Jammu and Kashmir and Madras. In most other States, the concessions given in free studentships at the secondary stage have been increased very considerably and the stage seems to be well set for making all secondary education free in the next five to ten years. Even at the university stage, there is a strong pressure to make education free or to reduce fees to the minimum. In Jammu and Kashmir, university education is free for all. In some other States such as Maharashtra or Gujarat, there are very large concessions of free studentships at the university stage and the trend to expand these concessions is continually on the increase. Fees in higher education have come to be stabilized at a low level and any attempt to raise them is vigorously resisted. If the recent developments in Mysore are any guide, it has also become politically impossible to raise them to any substantial extent."

III   *India's Quantitative Educational Requirements*

The purpose of this chapter is to provide an interpretation of India's quantitative educational requirements.[1] This statement will constitute the basis for assessing, in the following chapter, the quantitative goals that have actually been established in the educational plans of the nation.

Given the limitations proposed for this investigation, the major concern of this chapter is with the problem of evaluating the consequences of alternative courses of educational development. As stated in the Introduction, these data will be obtained from an examination of India's experience with its educational system and the body of informed Indian opinion, which presumably would be indicative of the adequacy of the existing school system, and from a hypothetical formulation of the stages of educational development. Since the data relating to India's experience with and opinion of its educational system may be viewed as providing confirmatory evidence for the hypothesis, the discussion of the hypothesis will be given first.

Before this hypothesis can be dealt with, however, it will be necessary to examine in more detail the relationship between education and national development. Although it was indicated in the Introduction that this relationship would be assumed—as it is in the educational plans—a more careful analysis is essential to an understanding of the choices presented by alternative quantitative educational objectives.

Education and National Development

Several economically oriented approaches that may be used in discussing a nation's quantitative educational requirements have al-

---

[1] Expressions such as "quantitative educational requirements" and "quantitative educational goals" will be used hereafter in reference to the basic problem of determining *how much* education should be provided. See above, p. 6.

ready been elaborated.[2] But these approaches generally treat education as an economic investment or a prerequisite for achieving a given rate of economic growth, and thus constitute an insufficient basis for making educational decisions. National development presumably entails other changes than those which are directly related to the economy; these must also be considered in the determination of a country's educational objectives.[3]

It is also pertinent to point out that in applying most of these theoretical approaches, the proponents of these approaches do not accept the relationship of education to economic growth, but rather are concerned with establishing this connection. Those using the so-called "correlation" approach, for example, explicitly attempt to demonstrate an association between education and economic growth. Similarly, users of the "residual" approach, after showing that a significant part of economic growth cannot be explained by increases in the quantity of labor and capital, usually suggest that education is an important constituent of the "residual" factor responsible for the unexplained growth, but cannot provide further evidence of the connection with this method. Those applying the "rate-of-returns" approach have as their objective the discovery of how the incomes earned by individuals who possess varying amounts of education are related to the monetary costs of obtaining the educational qualifications involved; conceivably, this approach could lead to the conclusion that education had little or no effect. Among the major approaches, only in the "manpower" approach is the relationship of education to economic growth definitely assumed.

[2] For a general review and critique of these techniques, see, for example, John Vaizey (1962, pp. 37–53); William G. Bowen (1964, pp. 3–38); Alice M. Rivlin (1962, pp. 360–378); Frederick Harbison and Charles A. Myers (1964, pp. 3–11); Jo W. Saxe (1963, pp. 49–55); Mary Jean Bowman (1964, pp. 3–7); and Thomas Balogh (1964, pp. 5–17). Additional relevant literature is cited in the following bibliographies: Marian C. Alexander-Frutschi (1963); Mark Blaug (1966); and *Educational Planning: A Bibliography* (1964).

[3] To be sure, the broader requirements of national development have not been entirely ignored in these approaches. See, for example, the treatment of the "cultural approach" in Herbert Parnes (1962, pp. 63–65).

The benefits of any quantitative educational objective derive from its relationship to some further end. However, as an intermediate goal approaches more closely to an ultimate goal, the relationship becomes less precise. It is difficult to state, for example, what measures are necessary to achieve an ultimate goal such as "national development." The generally accepted solution to this problem is to attempt to express the ultimate end in operational terms, recognizing that it is fundamentally a matter of interpretation and judgment whether this specification is an adequate statement of the ultimate objective. See Herbert A. Simon (1948, pp. 176–177); James G. March and Herbert A. Simon (1958, pp. 155–157); Roland N. McKean (1958, pp. 28–34); Charles J. Hitch and Roland N. McKean (1960, pp. 160–164).

Yet the *potential* contribution of education to national development does not seem to be open to serious argument. Many societies have found the outcomes of schooling to be desirable, and it is for this reason that educational systems have been established and are maintained. Indeed, if education by definition is a means of effecting changes in human behavior, the only questions that should be asked are whether the appropriate kinds and quantities of education are being used to accomplish the intended learning outcomes, whether the outcomes sought are the most suitable, and whether the results achieved justify the costs.

In order to specify the relationship between education and national development, it will be necessary, therefore, to look more closely at the functions of schools in a society. The following principal educational function may be identified: the accomplishment of behavioral change in order to prepare individuals for adult roles in society. In short, education exists to bring about desired role performances.

A "role" may be defined as a differentiated position within a social structure. An individual would normally fill several roles; for example, he may be a member of a family, a worker in a particular occupation, and a citizen. This definition is relatively broad and nontechnical, conforming closely to that given by Levy, who has used "role" to mean

> any position differentiated in terms of a given social structure whether the position be institutionalized or not. A given role is the classification of the social position given to the individual who performs an activity differentiated in terms of the social structure. These roles involve obligations, rights, and expected performances of the individuals who hold them. The positions of thief, doctor, outcast, injured man, etc. are all roles in this sense. A distinction may be drawn between *ideal* and *actual* roles. An *ideal* role is an *institutionalized role*. Such a role involves normative standards, conformity with which is generally to be expected, and failure to conform with which is met by moral indignation. An *actual role* is the position in fact occupied by an individual. It is what he in fact does with regard to any socially differentiated position whether institutionalized or not.[4]

In all societies, because of the continuous replacement of an older generation by a younger one, it is necessary for the new members of the society to learn how to perform effectively in the roles they will enter as adults. This process, called socialization, may be

[4] Marion J. Levy (1952, pp. 159–160).

accomplished without the assistance of formal educational institutions. However, school systems have been established in many societies as the most efficient means for imparting some of the learnings that are required for adult roles. To illustrate this point, let it be assumed that in a particular role the learnings needed for the effective performance of that role may be acquired either through schooling or some alternative such as trial-and-error learning. The principal cost of schooling is the loss represented by the time that the teacher and the students are withdrawn from productive work (the cost of facilities is usually a much less important factor). However, the learner would presumably spend more time if he learned through trial and error, and with much less certainty that he would ultimately acquire the desired learnings. Thus the major additional cost involved in formal schooling is the cost of the teacher, but this might well be offset by the greater chance that the learner will reach the desired level of role performance and the shorter length of time required.

In a static society, therefore, with a given number of roles and levels of role performance, the decision regarding how many persons to educate would be determined on the basis of the relative costs and benefits of substituting schooling for other methods of acquiring the required learnings. In a society undergoing change, however, the existing quantum of schooling (if any) combined with the learnings acquired through other means may not suffice to bring about the kinds of role performance desired; formal instruction may then be substituted for informal learning not only because of the greater efficiency of the former, but also in order to achieve levels or types of role performance that cannot be achieved without it. The expense of providing the education necessary to achieve these new role performances would represent an additional cost that is compensated by the greater benefits that are obtained. This is the consideration that appears to be operative as a country moves from a traditional role structure (where little formal schooling may be justified) to the role structure required of a modern technological society, in which a highly developed school system seems an essential element.

The Stages of Educational Development

With the aid of the concept of role performance and data from countries which have already established modern educational systems, a general hypothesis describing the appropriate quantitative requirements at different stages of educational development may be formulated.[5] Since a modernizing society might not have, or would

[5] For an earlier statement of this hypothesis and its application to a typology of the world's educational systems, see John A. Laska (1964, pp. 251–263).

presumably not be willing to devote, sufficient resources to introduce immediately a complete educational system modeled after that found in the most advanced countries, such a society would, if maximum benefits were desired, develop first the level or levels of the school system which yield the greatest returns. In a nation without previously existing schools, the problem of choice would emerge in its clearest form. As its first priority, such a society would face a limited number of alternatives: its resources could be initially concentrated on either primary, secondary, or university education, or on two or more educational levels.[6] The latter alternative covers the possibility that the development of two or more levels of the school system may be equally desirable; it does not refer to the fact that the successful expansion of one level may be dependent upon the previous development of other levels. For example, in order to establish a program in higher education it would obviously first be necessary to develop the primary and secondary levels, but the provision of primary and secondary schooling could not in this case be regarded as having a priority for its own sake. Similarly, the expansion of one level of an educational system in order to supply teachers for another must be considered to reflect the placement of a priority on the level which ultimately uses the teachers, not on both.

The decision regarding which educational level, if any, to emphasize first and regarding the extent to which it should be developed requires an analysis of the relative costs and benefits involved. Education, as has been suggested above, contributes to national development by changing human behavior and, consequently, role performances. In every modern society there is a wide variation in the value to the society of performances in different roles. Incumbents in a small number of roles—higher government officials and members of the professions, for instance—have, through their role performances, a significant effect upon the welfare of all members of the society. It follows that if these critical role performances were improved only slightly, the cumulative benefits to the society would be considerable, compared to the benefits that would result from expending the equivalent amount of resources on persons filling less important roles.

How much education should be provided to the potential incumbents in these vital roles? For many of them, education at the

---

[6] Although for convenience the development of the educational system is referred to in stating these alternatives, strictly speaking it is the development of educated persons in the society which is meant. The educational institutions utilized for this purpose would not have to be physically located in the country under consideration, but this would usually be true for primary and secondary level education, at least. Schools located in another country, while not a part of the developing society's educational system administratively, could correctly be regarded as a functional component.

university level would appear to be essential. In some roles (such as the professions) university or equivalent education is usually a prerequisite for even a minimum level of performance. For many of the others, education at the university level, though more costly than primary or secondary schooling, would seem to yield a higher ratio of benefits to costs.[7]

The first stage in the development of an educational system, therefore, would require the provision of university level education, both general and professional, to a limited number of persons. As indicated above, placing first priority on this level would necessitate a sufficient quantity of primary and secondary schooling to insure an adequate supply of students for the university level. During this stage of educational development, it would also be necessary to give a certain number of persons a secondary-level education to prepare them for the subordinate roles, such as those of clerk and technician, that must be filled for maximum effectiveness to be obtained from the role performances of the university graduates, and for the other important roles in which a secondary education gives a higher ratio of benefits to costs than primary schooling.[8] The amount of secondary education (both general and vocational) needed in the first stage would, however, also seem to be limited.[9]

As the marginal returns from the initial development of the university and secondary levels declined, a point would be reached where the benefits that could be obtained from offering education at these levels to an additional person would be equivalent to the value that would result from putting the same resources into the development of the primary level. Thereafter, all three levels of the school system would expand in accordance with their relative marginal benefits-costs relationships. Assuming that the experience of the advanced nations is relevant to that of the underdeveloped societies, the total provision of university- and secondary-level education would still be in limited quantity at the time universal primary schooling was at-

[7] The calculation of the social returns to education is extremely difficult. Yet, in making educational decisions at the national level, an evaluation of societal benefits is necessary. Perhaps the only feasible method now available is to reduce the problem to specific instances. Various roles would be identified, the incremental benefits attributable to education that could be derived from a given role performance would be specified, and judgments obtained as to whether a given amount of education (at a certain cost) was justified. See John Vaizey (1962, pp. 46–49); Richard S. Eckhaus (1962); Mary Jean Bowman (1962, pp. 647–659); Herbert Parnes (1962, pp. 39–41, 63–65).

[8] Some education for these purposes would also be required at the higher education level in other than university and equivalent institutions.

[9] The specific quantity of education at the university and secondary levels that would be required is discussed on pp. 44–47. It is assumed, of course, that a sufficient number of the persons educated for certain roles actually enter those roles.

tained.[10] Thus the second stage of educational development would involve the achievement of universal primary education, but not universal secondary schooling.

The third stage would follow logically from the second, entailing the vertical expansion of school enrollments by raising the school-leaving age and providing, in effect, universal secondary education. During this period educational opportunity at the highest level would also increase. The precise sequence of events cannot be postulated in detail, however, because the problems of this stage are of a different order from those of the two preceding stages.[11]

Empirical Referents of the Hypothesis

It is now necessary to introduce appropriate empirical referents for the above hypothesis, by means of which the hypothesis may be applied and predictions of consequences deduced. Ideally, these empirical referents would relate to the proportions of persons in a society who are successfully completing each of the three principal educational levels. Such measures of educational performance, which will be called completion ratios, may be obtained by comparing the number of students finishing an educational level with the total population in the relevant age group (the age group which corresponds to the average age of those graduating).

This method of determining the proportion of persons in a particular age group who complete a specified educational level is valid only in a stable situation, where significant fluctuations in the proportions of the various age groups represented in the population of graduates do not occur. Its justification lies in the fact that it entails a comparison of two population streams moving at equivalent rates (one grade or one age interval per year). Where information on the number of students promoted from a particular grade cannot be obtained, the total enrollment in the grade may be substituted. An enrollment ratio, however, would indicate only the maximum rate of completion that is possible.[12] In the present study, when an enrollment

---

[10] See below, p. 45.

[11] The achievement of the first two stages would result in a fairly gross adjustment between the educational system and the needs of society. In the third stage, as the utility of providing formal schooling approached its limit, a more refined analysis of the role of education in national development would be necessary, including such matters as the relationships between education and social class, and the function of the school in recognizing and fostering talent (that is, the non-educational as well as the strictly educational functions of the school system).

[12] It is thus possible to find enrollment ratios that are in excess of 100 percent, although a completion ratio could never be greater than 100 percent under stable conditions.

ratio is used in place of a completion ratio, it has been assumed that the two ratios correspond closely enough to warrant the interpretations given.

Only three measures of the extent of schooling in an educational system will be utilized as empirical referents: the completion ratios for grade IV, for the last grade of the full primary course, and for the last grade of the general secondary course. It is believed that criteria related to these three reference points will be adequate for the purpose of broadly indicating the success of an educational system in achieving the three major developmental stages. In most if not all educational systems, primary schooling comprises at least four years of study, but in several countries secondary education begins with the fifth year. Therefore, in order to determine the extent of primary schooling in all nations regardless of differences in the organization of their educational systems, it will be necessary to compare the last grade of primary school which is common to these systems, that is, grade IV. As four years of primary education is often regarded as the minimum necessary to insure a reasonable opportunity for permanent literacy, the grade IV completion ratio is in itself a meaningful indicator of the extent of primary schooling. In addition to this measure, it will also be necessary to analyze the completion ratio for the last grade of primary school as it exists functionally in the educational system under consideration, for access to the secondary level depends upon completion of the full primary course. The general secondary course, which has been selected to provide the third criterion, occupies a critical place in the structure of any educational system. Since it is the main avenue to university education, the number completing this course has a controlling effect on the size of university enrollments. The completion ratio for general secondary education will thus serve to indicate the maximum proportion of persons being educated at the university level, as well as affording a direct measure of the extent of this form of secondary schooling. Although there are some variations among nations in the length and quality of general secondary schooling, the functions of this course are essentially the same in all educational systems.

Of these three empirical criteria, the one most essential to the application of the hypothesis is the general secondary completion ratio. The output from the secondary level would need to be of a specified minimum amount before an educational system could be regarded as having achieved the first stage of its educational development, but until universal primary schooling is attained this figure could not exceed a certain maximum. A crude but reasonably satisfactory indication of the requirements of the modernizing societies for general secondary school graduates may be obtained from an examination of the outputs that appear to have been sufficient in the advanced societies even after universal primary education had been achieved. Many of the most modern countries of Western Europe (Table 15) had,

TABLE 15

General Secondary School Graduates in Relation to Population of the Relevant Age Group in Selected European Countries, 1955

Country	Percentage
Norway	9.5
Sweden	9
Belgium	8.5
France	7
Austria	6.5
Denmark	5
Netherlands	5
Switzerland	5
Great Britain	4.5
Germany (F. R.)	3.5

as late as 1955, a production of general secondary school graduates [13] that was only about from 4 to 10 percent of the relevant age group.[14] In other advanced nations this percentage has been correspondingly low. Japan, immediately before World War II, had an output from its secondary schools which was less than 2 percent,[15] while the USSR, as recently as 1954, graduated less than 10 percent.[16] The United States, which is the country that has achieved the greatest expansion of secondary education, did not surpass the 10 percent figure until after 1910.[17]

These data are useful in suggesting an order of magnitude. A modernizing country in the first and second stages of its educational development would seem to require a secondary school output that

[13] Because of the stated limitation of this measure to the graduates of general secondary schools, the modifier "general" will not be further employed.

[14] Hereafter, the expression "of the relevant age group" will be omitted, but it should be understood as applying to all percentages that are given.

[15] Completion figures obtained from data in Ronald S. Anderson (1959, pp. 36–37). See also Herbert Passin (1965, pp. 103–108).

[16] See Nicholas DeWitt (1961, p. 150).

[17] *Digest of Educational Statistics* (1963, p. 41). This completion ratio probably includes students in non-university-preparatory curriculums.

would approach but not exceed that which is found in the more advanced societies—perhaps a completion ratio of from 1 to 5 percent. There are several reasons why it is not possible to give a more exact figure. The proposed completion ratio must accommodate societies which have just entered Stage I of their educational development as well as countries completing Stage II. Also, this figure must have sufficient range of variation to allow for different levels of economic and social development in the countries concerned and for different role structures. Evaluations of the costs and benefits of the various types and quantities of education may also differ somewhat from one society to another. Another factor that would militate against a more precise completion ratio is the proportion of males represented in the total output from the secondary level: in nations in which most of the graduates of the secondary school are males, a figure of 2.5 percent, for example, would imply nearly 5.0 percent of the male population. Also, the number of secondary school graduates who will later become teachers and thus only serve to maintain the educational system has not been considered, although it is not believed that this factor would significantly affect the validity of the suggested figure, since only approximately 1 percent of the age group represented by the secondary school graduates would need to become teachers in order to maintain the educational systems of most countries. Finally, there may be variations in the educational structures of different countries—such as the presence or absence of schools which provide general education but do not lead to university entrance—that may affect the number of secondary school graduates required.

Therefore, a secondary level completion ratio of from 1 to 5 percent will be adopted as the criterion for an educational system that is either in Stage I or Stage II. Stage I will be distinguished from Stage II on the basis of the proportion of students completing primary school: Stage I would require a minimum amount of primary education whereas Stage II would, of course, entail universal primary schooling. In order to provide a sufficiently large number of primary school students to allow for wastage and to permit a selection for the secondary level, the number of students completing grade IV of the primary course in Stage I would probably need to be 10 to 20 times greater than the number constituting the desired secondary school output. But the output from grade IV could not be excessive either, if the first priority of producing university and secondary school graduates were to be met. Therefore, to establish another criterion, an educational system that is to be classified as Stage I should reach a secondary level completion ratio of 1 percent at least x years after the grade IV completion ratio has attained 20 percent (x is defined as the number of grades between grade IV and the last grade of the secondary course). Similarly, since a grade IV completion ratio of 50 percent should be able to provide for a 5 percent secondary school output, a 50 percent grade IV completion ratio will be regarded as the upper limit for a Stage I educational system. This latter figure is also appropriate as a criterion for differentiating between Stage I and Stage II in that it represents the half-way point toward achievement of the goal of universal primary schooling. The criteria for Stage I and for the other stages of educational development are summarized in Table 16.

TABLE 16
Criteria for Delimitation of Educational Development Stages

Stage of Educational Development	(1) Grade IV Completion Ratio	(2) Primary Level Completion Ratio	(3) Secondary Level Completion Ratio
Prior to Stage I	Less than 20 percent	—[a]	With (1) less than 20 percent, less than 1 percent x years later [b]
Stage I	Not more than 50 percent	—	At least 1 percent x years after (1) reaches 20 percent, but not to exceed 5 percent
Stage I Deviation	20 percent or more	—	Less than 1 percent x years after (1) achieved
Stage II	50 percent to 100 percent	No lower limit to 100 percent	1 percent to 5 percent
Stage II Deviation	—	Less than 100 percent	More than 5 percent while (2) less than 100 percent
Stage III	Approximately 100 percent	Approximately 100 percent	More than 5 percent

[a] Dash indicates irrelevant criterion.
[b] x is the number of grades between grade IV and the last grade of the secondary course.

Although the educational histories of most modernizing nations would reveal an early educational development that conforms to the proposed hypothesis, some countries appear to have expanded primary schooling without achieving a commensurate growth at the secondary level. This type of educational development, which will be termed Stage I Deviation, is characterized by a grade IV completion ratio of 20 percent or more and a secondary level output of less than 1 percent x years after the grade IV ratio is attained.

Having achieved Stage I and satisfied its minimum needs for highly educated persons, a nation in the second stage of its educational development would be directing its efforts toward the attainment of universal primary schooling. For the achievement of this stage the completion ratio for the full primary course becomes an important criterion, in addition to the completion ratios for grade IV and the secondary level. As long as the output from the secondary schools does not exceed 5 percent, an educational system will be considered to be in Stage II when completion ratios at the primary level vary from a minimum of 50 percent in grade IV to maximums of 100 percent in grade IV and the final grade of the primary course.[18] When approximately 100 percent are completing the full primary course, expansion of output from the secondary level could be resumed, inaugurating Stage III educational development. The precise determination of the point at which universal primary schooling is achieved involves an element of judgment, unless a rigorous standard is adhered to. In many situations a completion ratio of 80 percent in the final year of the primary course may seem appropriate; however, this figure will not be used as a criterion for Stage II.

Several countries have clearly departed from the postulated sequence of development in Stage II. After reaching Stage I these nations have increased the output from the secondary level to more than 5 percent without first achieving substantially universal schooling in the last grade of the primary level. Educational systems of this type will be identified as Stage II Deviation systems. Most nations experience few problems in attaining the first developmental stage; even the new countries of Africa whose previous educational growth had diverged from the priorities of Stage I are now rapidly overcoming their earlier deficiencies. An extremely difficult task for many contemporary societies as they attempt to move beyond Stage I, however, is that of restricting the further development of secondary education while at the same time increasing the amount of resources devoted to the primary level.

Nations undergoing the third stage of educational development would have a secondary level completion ratio in excess of 5 percent,

---

[18] A lower limit for the final grade of the primary course is not necessary. It should be noted that these criteria apply to the same year; the x factor used in Stage I delimitation is not applicable to either Stages II or III.

with universal schooling at the primary level having previously been attained in Stage II. Many of the countries of Europe since World War II appear to have entered this stage. Even better examples, however, are the United States, Japan, and perhaps the USSR, all of which have made significant progress toward the provision of expanded educational opportunities at the secondary and university levels. These countries also seem to have reached Stage III by progressing through the first two stages of educational development in the sequence hypothesized.

With the empirical referents for each of the postulated developmental stages, the hypothesis may be used for the prediction of consequences. In countries which have not yet achieved Stage I, it would be expected that the weight of informed opinion in the society would favor an increased provision of secondary and university level graduates. The weight of informed opinion in countries with Stage I or Stage II educational systems would be expected to advise a course of action compatible with the attainment of the next higher stage. Countries whose educational systems are classified as Stage I Deviation systems would presumably be experiencing a shortage of secondary and university level graduates. The opposite situation, however, would be expected in countries with systems undergoing Stage II Deviation; in these societies a number of secondary school and university graduates who are either unemployed or in jobs where their educational attainments are under-utilized would be anticipated.

Application of the Hypothesis to India

For a test of its predictive capability, the hypothesis will now be applied to the Indian educational system. In 1961 India had a grade V enrollment ratio [19] of 35.3 percent and a secondary level completion ratio of 7.5 percent (Table 29), thus indicating a Stage II Deviation educational system. However, because education in India is primarily a state responsibility, it is necessary to examine the situation in the various states. It is possible that some states might be in Stage III, and thus quite properly expanding their secondary level completion ratios, which, when combined with the lower ratios of other states, would still give a ratio for India of over 5 percent while the combined ratio for grade V would be less than 100 percent.

Table 17 reveals, however, that in 1961 only one state (Kerala) had a primary level enrollment ratio of 100 percent in the terminal

---

[19] Because the terminal grade of the primary level is grade IV or grade V in all of the Indian states, the use of one ratio seems appropriate in reference to the criteria for Stage II.

TABLE 17
States, Enrollment Ratios of Terminal Grades, Primary Level, 1961

State	Sex [a]	Enrollment, Last Full Grade [b] Primary Level	Population of Relevant Age Group [c]	Enrollment Ratio
Andhra Pradesh	MF	285,700 (V)	821,400	34.8
	M	190,700	411,700	46.3
Assam	MF	106,400 (V)	295,100	36.1
	M	71,200	150,700	47.2
Bihar	MF	265,200 (V)	1,092,100	24.3
	M	221,700	569,400	38.9
Gujarat	MF	264,100 (IV)	526,500	50.2
	M	177,500	271,200	65.4
Jammu and Kashmir	MF	27,400 (V)	82,800	33.1
	M	21,800	43,200	50.5
Kerala	MF	422,100 (IV)	419,300	100.7
	M	229,100	208,700	109.8
Madhya Pradesh	MF	196,900 (V)	710,700	27.7
	M	158,700	364,600	43.5
Madras	MF	395,500 (V)	738,600	53.5
	M	258,100	367,500	70.2
Maharashtra	MF	537,800 (IV)	957,400	56.2
	M	365,100	497,000	73.5
Mysore	MF	280,100 (IV)	560,100	50.0
	M	186,600	282,000	66.2
Orissa	MF	65,500 (V)	406,400	16.1
	M	55,700	201,200	27.7
Punjab	MF	214,700 (V)	515,400	41.7
	M	156,700	272,500	57.5
Rajasthan	MF	110,600 (V)	493,300	22.4
	M	91,800	255,200	36.0
Uttar Pradesh	MF	437,700 (V)	1,697,000	25.8
	M	356,700	879,600	40.6
West Bengal	MF	399,400 (IV)	841,600	47.5
	M	238,400	426,800	55.9

[a] MF = males and females; M = males only.
[b] Roman numerals in parentheses denote grades involved.
[c] Relevant age groups as follows: grade IV, age 10; grade V, age 11.

grade. Since the corresponding enrollment ratios of the other states did not exceed 56.2 percent, none of these states—if their course of educational development were to conform to the hypothesis given above—should have had secondary level completion ratios of more than 5 percent.[20] Even if the primary enrollment ratio for males is considered, the highest ratio (with the exception of Kerala) is only 73.5 percent, which represents less than universal primary schooling.

On the other hand, as shown in Table 18, only three states (Andhra Pradesh, Madhya Pradesh, and Orissa) had secondary level completion ratios of less than 5 percent (two were over 4 percent). Only these states—which would be classified as Stage I [21]—and Kerala —which would be classified as Stage III—did not exhibit Stage II Deviation. Thus it seems correct to regard the Indian school system as falling into the category of systems undergoing Stage II Deviation. This classification suggests, therefore, that India in 1961 had too much general secondary and university education in relation to the quantity of schooling provided at the primary level.

Quantitative Educational Requirements: Indian Experience and Opinion

It now remains to ascertain whether the predicted consequences of Stage II Deviation actually obtain in India. One of the most striking indications of an apparent excess of general secondary and university education in relation to the amount of schooling at the primary level in India is provided by the phenomenon of "educated unemployment." The difficulty of educated Indians in securing employment commensurate with their training was an early outcome of the rapid growth of university education after 1857. By the 1880's "unemployment had become chronic among the educated class." [22] The increase in the number of employment opportunities available after World War I was unable to relieve this situation; between 1919 and 1936, no less than eleven government committees published reports which dealt with educated unemployment.[23] It was estimated in one of these reports that "only 20 percent of the educated classes have employment in keeping with the standard of their educational qualifications," while from 60 to 70 percent had "inadequate employment," and 10 to 15 percent were unemployed.[24]

The problem of educated unemployment has continued to be a

[20] Universal primary schooling is a relatively recent achievement in Kerala. In 1957 the grade IV enrollment ratio was approximately 90 percent.
[21] If the completion ratios for males are considered separately, only Orissa would be classified as Stage I, and just barely so.
[22] See Bruce T. McCully (1940, p. 196).
[23] See Walter Kotschnig (1937, p. 80).
[24] *Ibid.*, p. 130.

TABLE 18
States, Secondary Level Completion Ratios, 1961

State	Sex [a]	Number Passing School Leaving Examination (Matriculation)	Population of Relevant Age Group [b]	Completion Ratio
Andhra Pradesh	MF	34,430	746,000 (16)	4.6
	M	29,560	372,300	7.9
Assam	MF	13,350	245,400 (16)	5.4
	M	10,940	126,300	8.7
Bihar	MF	51,190	881,400 (16)	5.8
	M	47,450	455,300	10.4
Gujarat [c]	MF	41,360	428,800 (16)	9.6
	M	32,320	223,200	14.5
Jammu and Kashmir	MF	4,720	72,800 (16)	6.5
	M	3,680	38,200	9.6
Kerala	MF	47,290	366,500 (15)	12.9
	M	30,030	178,500	16.8
Madhya Pradesh	MF	25,090	598,900 (16)	4.2
	M	21,500	306,900	7.0
Madras	MF	44,250	686,400 (16)	6.4
	M	34,600	337,200	10.3
Maharashtra	MF	66,760	791,700 (16)	8.4
	M	49,630	414,500	12.0
Mysore	MF	34,150	496,800 (16)	6.9
	M	27,920	247,400	11.0
Orissa	MF	8,810	348,600 (16)	2.5
	M	8,080	175,900	4.6
Punjab	MF	64,970	429,300 (16)	15.1
	M	48,520	227,500	21.3
Rajasthan	MF	23,840	417,500 (16)	5.7
	M	21,340	219,400	9.7
Uttar Pradesh	MF	104,280	1,524,300 (15)	6.8
	M	88,180	805,800	10.9
West Bengal	MF	52,260	706,900 (16)	7.4
	M	39,690	371,400	10.7

[a] MF = males and females; M = males only.
[b] Figures in parentheses denote ages involved.
[c] Enrollment in grade XI given in place of number passing the school leaving examination.

serious one in post-independence India. A nation-wide sample survey conducted in late 1955 revealed that 12.9 percent of the matriculates residing in urban areas were unemployed; the unemployment rate for both arts graduates and science graduates was 7.9 percent.[25] In a follow-up study of 1954 university graduates, 15.1 percent of the arts graduates, 7.1 percent of the science graduates, and 7.0 percent of the commerce graduates responding to a questionnaire stated they were unemployed in 1960.[26]

Also significant in indicating the excessive quantities of university graduates in arts, science, and commerce is the evidence that a large proportion of them are employed in clerical and other subordinate occupations. It is generally assumed in India that a secondary level education affords a sufficient preparation for a clerical occupation, yet in 1955 according to the sample survey referred to above, 30.2 percent of the science graduates and 40.1 percent of the arts graduates were employed in clerical and other subordinate occupations.[27] Similar data were obtained in the survey of 1954 university graduates; it was found that 24.4 percent of the arts graduates, 20.0 percent of the science graduates, and 43.4 percent of the commerce graduates were employed as clerks.[28]

The Union Ministry of Education has responded to the problem of educated unemployment by advocating a policy of restricted and selective admission to the universities and a policy of diversification of education at the secondary level (which, by providing increased opportunities for vocational education, would presumably reduce the pressures for expansion of general secondary education). In 1953, for example, Maulana Azad, the Union Minister of Education, stated that

[25] Pitambar Pant and T. P. Chaudhuri (1959, p. 36).

[26] India, Directorate General of Employment and Training, *Report on the Pattern of Graduate Employment* (New Delhi: Directorate General of Employment and Training, 1963), p. 50. (Draft; mimeographed.)

[27] Pitambar Pant and T. P. Chaudhuri (1959, pp. 32–33). It may be objected that with a combined university-preparatory and university course of only fourteen to fifteen years' duration in most states, a person with a bachelor's degree is not inappropriately in a clerical occupation. However, as long as a bachelor's degree is generally regarded in India as constituting an adequate preparation for superior administrative positions and a secondary level education deemed sufficient for clerical occupations, the self-evident wastefulness of using university graduates in the latter roles must be insisted upon. If a large number of Indian university graduates are in fact unsuitable for more demanding occupations, this must be held to be a fault of the process whereby students are selected for admission to the university, rather than the length of study involved. In an educational system in which 1–2 percent of the relevant age group acquire a bachelor's degree, this small group should comprise the most talented proportion of the population. If fourteen years of study is adequate to prepare some of this group for elite roles, it should be sufficient for the remainder.

[28] India, Directorate General of Employment and Training, *Report on the Pattern of Graduate Employment,* Table 5 (4).

> . . . the most important consideration for the reform of university education appears to be to limit the number of students. . . . We have to ensure that with the expansion of elementary and secondary education there is no inordinate increase in these numbers.

Secondary education, Azad declared:

> . . . must be for the majority the entrance to life in various industries, crafts, and professions and serve as an entrance to higher education only for a select minority. . . . If we are to . . . provide that the majority seek such professions at the end of secondary . . . education, it is necessary to reorganize secondary education to provide for a variety of diversified courses.[29]

The Union Minister of Education in 1959, K. L. Shrimali, reaffirmed this policy, noting that the Government of India had come to the conclusion that

> . . . at the University stage, admissions should both be selective and restricted. . . . While restriction of admission to the universities has become an urgent need, steps will have to be taken simultaneously to make Secondary education more practical so that it may be a terminal point for the majority of students.[30]

Other Indian officials have advocated similar policies. In 1957, the Chairman of the University Grants Commission, C. D. Deshmukh, said:

[29] India, Ministry of Education, *Central Advisory Board of Education (1935–1960): Silver Jubilee Souvenir* (Delhi: Manager of Publications, 1960), pp. 283–284.

[30] India, Ministry of Education, *Proceedings of the Second [Fourth] State Education Ministers' Conference* (Delhi: Manager of Publications, 1960), p. 6.

See also the recommendations of the Secondary Education Commission for the establishment of multipurpose high schools, above, pp. 28, 29. Even where multipurpose schools have been established, however, they have not been able to halt the rush of students to the universities. The basic reasons for this failure are not difficult to discover. Students will be attracted to vocationally oriented programs instead of the university only when they are offered the prospect of a career that is as satisfying as what they might achieve after completion of university education. These prospects do not exist in contemporary India. Students might still be induced to take vocational courses for want of a better alternative if the level of performance required in the university-preparatory course were such that few could attain this standard, or if a system of selection rigidly limited the number of students who could be admitted to the academic course. But these conditions have generally not been imposed on the Indian educational system (see the discussion of selection, above, pp. 30–36); consequently, the hopes of the Secondary Education Commission have not been realized.

We shall have to restrict University education by and large to the number of university educated men and women that the country will be needing from time to time and that as regards the rest, the nation will have done its duty by expanding and extending as well as diversifying Secondary education.[31]

The Study Group on Educated Unemployed was set up by the Planning Commission in 1955 in order to assess the extent of unemployment among educated persons and to develop proposals for ameliorating the situation. Among the Study Group's recommendations was the following:

What we plead is for a deliberate and reasoned expansion [of educational facilities] in those directions in which the need is demonstrable while discouraging growth in those sectors which only help to keep uneasy young men out of the employment market for some years more.[32]

More recently, J. P. Naik, a member of the Education Commission, has urged that

. . . at the secondary stage, our first attempt [in the formulation of a new enrollment policy] should be to restrict the extremely rapid and indiscriminate expansion of general secondary education that is now taking place.[33]

The need to achieve universal primary schooling has, if anything, been even more strongly asserted than the desirability of restricting the growth of general secondary and university education. Article 45 of the Constitution, which is contained in Part IV, Directive Principles of State Policy, provides as follows:

The State shall endeavour to provide, within a period of ten years from the commencement of this Constitution, for free and compulsory education for all children until they complete the age of fourteen years . . . . [while] the provisions contained in this Part shall not be enforceable by any court, [they] are nevertheless fundamental in the governance of the country and it shall be the duty of the State to apply these principles in making laws.[34]

[31] India, Ministry of Education, *Indian University Administration* (Delhi: Manager of Publications, 1958), p. 16.
[32] India, Planning Commission, *Outline Report of the Study Group on Educated Unemployed* (Delhi: Manager of Publications, 1956), p. 50.
[33] See J. P. Naik (1965, Paper No. 3, p. 43).
[34] Part IV, Article 37. "State" is defined in the Constitution to include "the Government and Parliament of India and the Government and the Legislature of each of the States and all local or other authorities within the territory of India or under the control of the Government of India" (Part III, Article 12).

When it became evident that Article 45 would not be implemented within ten years of its adoption (that is, by 1960) as stipulated, the Education Panel of the Planning Commission recommended at its meeting in July, 1957, that the time limit be extended to 1965–66 and that free and compulsory schooling be provided for all children up to the age of eleven rather than fourteen.[35] This proposal was endorsed by the conference of state ministers of education held in September, 1957, and also by the Central Advisory Board of Education in February, 1958.[36]

These two views of India's educational situation—that universal primary schooling ought to be achieved and that the quantity of general secondary and university education is more than adequate—have also been combined in recommendations for the establishment of priorities for the growth of the school system. Maulana Azad, the first Union Minister of Education, in his address to the Central Advisory Board of Education in January, 1950, spoke of the need "to fix an order of priority, so that our limited resources are not frittered away in attempting too many things simultaneously." First among the objectives which Azad enumerated was the provision of primary education on "a universal, free and compulsory basis"; the expansion of secondary and university education, on the other hand, was not included in Azad's list of priorities.[37] On the state level, a legislative committee of the Madras government in a report prepared in 1956 emphasized the importance of adhering to an order of priority in educational development. The "expansion of numbers in standards [grades] VI to XI . . . should be regarded as subordinate to the requirements" of the program to attain universal primary schooling in grades I to V.[38]

Conclusions

It is clear, therefore, that at least an important segment of informed Indian opinion has interpreted the nation's educational experience to mean that an excessive number of general secondary school and university graduates was being produced in relation to the number

[35] India, Ministry of Education, *Proceedings of the [Third] State Education Ministers' Conference* (Delhi: Manager of Publications, 1958), p. 37.

[36] *Ibid.*, pp. 4–5; India, Ministry of Education, *Central Advisory Board of Education (1935–1960): Silver Jubilee Souvenir*, p. 363.

[37] India, Ministry of Education, *Central Advisory Board of Education (1935–1960): Silver Jubilee Souvenir*, p. 233.

[38] *Report of the Legislature Committee on White Paper on Education, Madras State, 1956* (Madras: Superintendent, Government Press, 1958), p. 7. "In recent years," the Committee pointed out, "progress has been taking place mainly in response to local demand; which is not necessarily the same as local need."

completing primary school. Accordingly, while calling for the attainment of universal primary schooling, a restriction on the expansion of the higher levels of the educational system has been advocated. Until the goal of universal primary schooling is achieved, no significant increase in general secondary and university education has been considered desirable.[39] This enrollment policy conforms to what has been indicated would be expected in a Stage II Deviation educational system.

The evidence supplied by India's educational experience and the weight of informed opinion in the nation thus support the hypothesis advanced above, which in turn—because it furnishes a prediction and logical explanation of the observed consequences—lends additional credence to the interpretation based on these data. It is now necessary to determine whether this interpretation of India's quantitative educational requirements has been accepted as the basis for the country's educational planning.

[39] At least this was true of the period 1947–1961. For a discussion of the views of the recent Education Commission, see below, pp. 116–117.

IV *Educational Planning: Goals*

Since its attainment of independence in 1947, India has produced four educational plans that fulfill the criteria specified as necessary to warrant consideration in this investigation. Three of these plans are components of the country's five-year plans, which have been prepared since 1951. The fourth plan, known as the Kher Committee Report, was published in 1950. A fifth document—the Central Advisory Board of Education Plan of 1944—must also be added to this group, because it was officially accepted for planning purposes by the Government of India and continued in effect during the first few years of the post-independence period.

The purpose of this chapter is to assess the degree to which the quantitative objectives and priorities indicated in these plans conform to India's educational requirements, as described in the chapter preceding. Because of the importance of accurately presenting the views of the planners, direct quotations will be extensively utilized.

Central Advisory Board of Education Plan

Comprehensive national educational planning in India began with the plan published by the Central Advisory Board of Education in 1944 under the title *Post-War Educational Development in India.*[1] That this document was explicitly regarded as a plan is indicated in the statement of its purpose: "The primary object of this report is to place a practicable plan of post-war development before the Reconstruction Committee of the Viceroy's Executive Council."[2] Prem Kirpal, Educational Advisor to the Government of India in 1960, has also affirmed that "the modern movement for educational planning in India began with the [CABE] Plan of 1944."[3]

[1] India, Bureau of Education, *Post-War Educational Development in India,* A Report by the Central Advisory Board of Education, January, 1944 (5th ed.; Delhi: Manager of Publications, 1947).
[2] *Ibid.,* p. 1.
[3] India, Ministry of Education, *Central Advisory Board of Education (1935–1960): Silver Jubilee Souvenir,* p. iii.

The CABE's plan, which was the outcome of a decade of attention to the problem of how to improve India's educational system, put forward a design for a school system that could be completed within forty years.[4] At the end of this period, the following quantitative objectives would be achieved: 100 percent of the relevant age group would receive eight years of education, 20 percent would graduate from high school after eleven years of study, and one out of ten to fifteen of the high school graduates would be selected for admission to the universities. The CABE considered education to be an essential prerequisite for national development and on this basis justified the amounts of schooling prescribed in the plan:

> The minimum provision which could be accepted as constituting a national system postulates that all children must receive enough education to prepare them to earn a living as well as fulfil themselves as individuals and discharge their duties as citizens. It also requires that those with the requisite capacity should be . . . trained to fill positions of responsibility in all walks of life.[5]

In advocating the establishment of universal primary education, the CABE argued that other countries had achieved this goal, and therefore India must do likewise. Universal primary schooling was also essential for a democracy. "The primary requisite of any system of public education for a democracy," the CABE declared, "is that it should provide for all its members, and not for a few only, at least such training as may be necessary to make them reasonably good citizens."[6] To attain this objective, the CABE felt that eight years of schooling were necessary, to be provided in a primary course of five years (junior basic school) followed by a higher elementary course of three years (senior basic school) for those students who did not gain admission to high school.

[4] The importance of education in national development and the need to eliminate the deficiencies of the existing school system were an early concern of the Board. At the first meeting of the CABE in 1935, following its reconstitution in that year, the Chairman, Girja Shankar Bajpai, emphasized that "education goes to the very root of individual contentment and national prosperity; neglect it, and there will be neither national prosperity nor individual contentment." The first item on the Board's agenda at this meeting—and the one which Bajpai considered of primary importance—was "Unemployment and Educational Reconstruction." The linking of the two topics was intentional. "No exceptional perspicacity is needed," Bajpai asserted, "to discern that this evil [educated unemployment] must largely result from the system of education. . . . The educationist [therefore] must not be afraid to mend the system to the extent that he can." *Ibid.*, pp. 14–15.

[5] India, Bureau of Education, *Post-War Educational Development in India*, p. 2.

[6] *Ibid.*, p. 6.

The main function of the high school (20 percent of the age group would enter this six-year course after completion of junior basic school, and all would be expected to graduate) was conceived to be that of preparing talented individuals for vital occupational roles. This level, according to the CABE, was "to form an élite not for its own sake but for that of society." Most of the high school graduates were expected to obtain employment immediately after the completion of the course, without the need for additional schooling. The need for selective admission to the high school was stressed by the CABE. "Character and intelligence, which are the essential attributes of any élite, are not confined to any particular class in the community; hence the selective principle . . . is of the greatest importance." Only by permitting the most talented children to enter high school would be the best interest of society be served. The CABE pointed out:

> . . . since in future the cost of high school education will be met largely out of public funds and only partially from fees, every high school pupil will be to some extent a scholarship-holder and it is in the public interest to ensure that the pupils admitted are those most likely to take the fullest advantage of the education provided and so prove a remunerative investment on the part of the community.[7]

Enrollment at the university level was also to be guided by national needs. The plan called attention to the excessive production of university graduates. The universities had failed to

> . . . adjust their output to the capacity of the employment market to absorb it. . . . If a careful statistical survey were made of unemployment among University graduates, perhaps not more than 20 per cent. would be found absolutely unemployed, but the numbers of those inadequately or unsuitably employed would probably exceed 50 per cent. This means that only 30 per cent of the University products can be said to have secured employment of a type which is in keeping with their attainments or commensurate with the time and money which have been spent on their education.[8]

The CABE felt that there had been a general lack of planning in university education: ". . . both Central and Provincial [state] Governments have yielded to popular pressure in bringing Universities into existence." At the same time, because of inadequate financial support, the universities were dependent upon student and examination fees; therefore, "they can hardly be expected to put such restrictions on

7 *Ibid.*, pp. 18–21.
8 *Ibid.*, pp. 26–27.

admissions as would allow high standards to be maintained and the risks of educated unemployment to be minimised." The result of this uncontrolled expansion of university education was what the CABE called a "top-heavy" school system, with too few students enrolled at the lower levels in comparison with the enrollment in the universities. The training that many students received in the universities was of little benefit to society, because "jobs for which boys with an ordinary High School education would be adequately suited are taken by University graduates." Although the CABE conceded that when the proposed school system was fully established India would need more university education and not less than the amount currently being provided, "the growth of Universities should be in proportion to the expansion in the lower stages [levels] and conditional on the introduction of a sound selective process in higher education." The selection policy advocated by the CABE would result in "only about one in ten to fifteen of the high school leavers" going on to the universities.[9]

On the critical question of priorities for educational development —that is, the relative rates of expansion of the different levels of the school system during the forty-year period required for implementation of the plan—the position adopted by the CABE was that except for the necessity of commencing with the lowest grade in order to provide students for the upper grades, the plan should be implemented at a *uniform rate* for the primary, secondary, and university levels. However, because of the presence of an existing university structure with a capacity that was already too large relative to the lower levels of the school system, no increase in university enrollments would presumably take place until the output from the high schools was ten to fifteen times greater than the intake into the universities. The CABE specifically rejected the idea that the first five years of schooling should be instituted on a universal basis before the desired expansion of the secondary level was achieved. In order to maintain the principle of uniform expansion, the CABE held that "the progression should clearly be from area to area and not from age to age." [10]

The failure to establish priorities for educational development that took account of the marginal utilities of the various amounts of education provided by the three major levels of the school system is the most serious criticism that can be made of the quantitative objec-

---

[9] *Ibid.*, pp. 20, 26–27, 29.

[10] *Ibid.*, p. 3; see also Table F, pp. 111–112, which shows the contemplated expansion of faculty in junior basic schools (grades I–V), senior basic schools (grades VI–VIII), and high schools (grades VI–XI) during the plan period. The rates of increase depicted for these three levels are fundamentally the same.

tives of the CABE Plan. By insisting on the principle of uniform development, the plan would countenance substantial additional expansion of secondary-level enrollments before universal primary schooling was achieved. Yet, as unsuitable as it might have been because of this defect, the CABE Plan reflected a considerable understanding of India's educational situation. By stressing the overdevelopment of the existing school system at the university level and the necessity for this maladjustment to be corrected, the Board gave convincing evidence that the country's educational planners were not only aware of one of India's major educational problems but were also capable of applying this knowledge in the formulation of an educational plan.

The plan was, in fact, accepted as the basis for guiding India's educational development during the first year or two following the achievement of independence on August 15, 1947. At the CABE's meeting in January, 1947, C. Rajagopalachari, the Chairman, referred to the general approval accorded the plan:

> We have made the Plan and everybody has accepted it in India. . . . Not only has there been no controversy over it but it has been positively welcomed. The central government as well as the provincial [state] governments, the Press and the people have all accepted it as good and sound.

Rajagopalachari went on to describe the implementation of the plan, which had already begun:

> But the more difficult task of execution has commenced. . . . We have received concrete plans from most of the provincial governments. . . . Altogether we have now fairly definite and detailed acceptances on the part of all the provincial authorities, who are responsible in the main for the carrying out of this plan.

At its meeting held in January, 1948, the CABE included as items on its agenda the receipt of reports from the national and provincial governments "in regard to the recommendations of the Board on Post-War Educational Development in India." By the time of the next meeting a year later, the CABE's agenda contained an item on "the progress of the Educational Development Plans implemented or proposed to be implemented" by the national and provincial governments.[11] The dropping of the distinctive modifier "post-war" as applied to the plans for educational development apparently signified that the CABE's 1944 plan was no longer the only one in existence; a

[11] India, Ministry of Education, *Central Advisory Board of Education (1935–1960): Silver Jubilee Souvenir,* pp. 169, 189, 215.

second national plan had in fact been prepared during 1948 and was ready for consideration by the Board during this meeting.

The Kher Committee Report

In spite of Rajagopalachari's earlier declaration that the CABE Plan had been accepted throughout the country, dissatisfaction with the pace of development outlined in the plan soon became evident. A special conference of India's leading educational officials was convened by Maulana Azad, the national Minister of Education, in January, 1948, immediately after the meeting of the CABE. As Azad explained in his opening address, the purpose of the conference was to "chalk out our future programme of action." He affirmed that "the scheme of Post-war Educational Development prepared by the Central Advisory Board of Education has been accepted by the Central and Provincial [state] Governments," and that steps had been taken to implement the plan, but he was unwilling to wait forty years for the introduction of universal primary education:

> After the realisation of our independence, we cannot . . . be content with programmes which were considered adequate for the old regime. Thus, no one will for a moment tolerate today that forty years must elapse before the full scheme of basic education for all the inhabitants of this land can be implemented. In fact, even half that period will seem to many to savour of delay and procrastination. We must, therefore, devise measures by which the educational progress of this country can be so accelerated that we reach our objective within a much shorter time. . . . We must not, for a moment, forget that it is the birth-right of every individual to receive at least the basic education without which he cannot fully discharge his duties as a citizen.[12]

The conference membership supported Azad's viewpoint and passed a resolution calling for a substantial reduction in the time necessary for the establishment of universal primary schooling. While endorsing the proposal of the CABE Plan for eight years of compulsory education, the conference recommended that if it were not feasible because of financial and other reasons to provide the full amount, the institution of five years of compulsory schooling as a first step should be considered. In making this recommendation the conference was, of course, rejecting the stipulation of the CABE Plan that the develop-

[12] India, Ministry of Education, *Proceedings of the Educational Conference held at New Delhi in January, 1948* (Delhi: Manager of Publications, 1949), pp. 4–5.

ment of the school system should under no circumstances proceed from one level to the next. As a final measure, the conference decided to appoint a committee to examine the program of educational development in all the provinces and states of India and to make suggestions to ensure that educational development would not be curtailed by a lack of funds. The committee was designated the Committee on Ways and Means of Financing Education, but it is generally referred to as the Kher Committee, taking its name from B. G. Kher, who was elected chairman at its first meeting.

The report of the Kher Committee, which was considered by the CABE in its January, 1949, session and published in 1950, is important for the indication it gives that the concept of restricted access to the secondary and university levels advocated in the CABE Plan continued to represent the thinking of Indian educational planners during the initial years of the post-independence period. Its proposals, the Committee declared, were "based on the assumption that 20% of the pre-Secondary children will go in for High School education," which was identical with the percentage given in the CABE Plan. The proportion of high school–leavers expected to enter the universities, which was set at one in ten, also conformed to the previous plan.[13]

But the major significance of the Kher Committee's plan was in its recognition of the need to give major emphasis to the expansion of primary schooling. Taking its inspiration from the education conference that had appointed it, the Committee recommended that

> . . . the programme of compulsory Basic Education . . . be limited to a period of about 5 years and not 8 years, as recommended in the Report of the Central Advisory Board of Education. The introduction of compulsory Junior Basic Education for the children of 6–11 [6–10] within a period of 10 years must receive *top priority* in any Government scheme of Educational Development. If financial conditions compel, the programme may be extended over a larger period, but in no circumstances should it be given up.[14]

The Committee recommended, therefore, that universal compulsory primary schooling of five grades be introduced within ten years by means of two five-year plans. Compulsion was to be extended to the age group 11–13 by the end of a third five-year plan.[15] In declar-

---

[13] India, Ministry of Education, *Report of the Committee on the Ways and Means of Financing Educational Develoment in India* (Delhi: Manager of Publications, 1950), p. 2.

[14] *Ibid.*, p. 5. (Emphasis supplied.)

[15] *Ibid.*, pp. 2, 26–27.

ing that "this responsibility must be undertaken without . . . detriment to the *existing* facilities for Secondary and Higher Education," the Committee seemed to oppose any expansion at the upper levels of the school system (except for the "provision of such higher studies as will be necessary for increasing the agricultural and industrial potential of the country") until primary schooling had been made universal.[16]

At the meeting of the CABE in January, 1949, Maulana Azad expressed his agreement with the Kher Committee's proposals, though he regretted that implementation of the complete plan could not begin immediately.

> The Ministry of Education have accepted this interim report and tried to provide funds in our next year's budget on that basis. . . . It has not, however, been possible to provide for the entire amount. Much against my will, I have been compelled to agree to a proposal to postpone consideration of this scheme for the time being.[17]

After consideration of the report, the CABE also gave its approval, but only after fundamental changes had been made in the text of the document.[18] One of these alterations resulted in the elimination of the word "existing" from the excerpt quoted above, making the phrase concerned read, "without . . . detriment to facilities for Secondary and Higher Education." By taking out the word "existing," unlimited expansion of the secondary and university levels would now seem to be permitted, whereas the original report would presumably have held enrollments at these levels stable (at least so far as general education was concerned) until all children of the relevant age group were entering primary school. A second change brought about the complete removal of the following sentence, also quoted above: "If financial conditions compel, the programme may be extended over a longer period, but in no circumstances should it be given up." This alteration, by eliminating the qualification proposed by the Committee, had the effect of insisting that universal primary schooling of five years' duration would definitely be provided within ten years. If this were to be accomplished "without detriment" to the expansion of education at the higher levels of the school system, it would imply that the full 1944 plan was to be completed within ten years instead of the forty

[16] *Ibid.*, p. 5. (Emphasis supplied.) The table presented on pp. 26–27 indicates that no increase in post-primary enrollments would take place until 100 per cent of the relevant age group were enrolled in grade I.

[17] India, Ministry of Education, *Central Advisory Board of Education (1935–1960): Silver Jubilee Souvenir*, p. 209.

[18] *Ibid.*, pp. 218–219.

initially specified. In view of Azad's earlier admission that the Kher Committee plan could not be put into effect by the central government until more financial resources became available, the action of the CABE in introducing these changes into the Kher Committee's recommendations seems most unrealistic.

Whether the national Ministry of Education accepted these modifications could not be determined. The published version of the plan contains the original text of the Kher Committee Report, without mention of the actions of the CABE. In this form, the Committee's document represented an important step forward in the preparation of a sound national plan. By substituting a set of priorities which stressed the rapid development of primary education in place of the "uniform development" advocated in the 1944 plan—while accepting the earlier plan's recognition of the need for selective admissions to the secondary and higher levels—the two basic elements necessary for a relatively optimal plan became available. Indeed, the only shortcoming of the Kher Committee Report was its failure to be adopted in its original version by the CABE (which would have meant gaining the support of the state governments represented on the Board). But as far as Indian educational planners were concerned, they had by 1950 ascertained the country's quantitative educational requirements and had produced an adequate educational plan. The stage, it would seem, had been set for the eventual incorporation of the essential elements of this plan into the comprehensive national five-year plans, which after 1951 became the principal vehicles for educational planning as well as for other types of social and economic planning.

The First Five-Year Plan

The creation of the Planning Commission in March, 1950, marked the effective beginning of comprehensive national planning in India. Much interest in the technique of national planning had preceded this event. In 1938, for example, the Congress Party set up a National Planning Committee, with Jawaharlal Nehru as its chairman. The war caused a disruption of its work, but a series of reports containing the findings of several subcommittees, including one on general education, was later published.[19] The British administration in India con-

[19] The establishment of the National Planning Committee is described in Jawaharlal Nehru, *Discovery of India* (1946, pp. 399–408). The report prepared by the subcommittee on general education, which had as its chairman S. Radhakrishnan, did not establish quantitative goals for educational development. A seven-year course of primary education was envisioned for the age group 7–13, but "at the end of the fifth year of basic education there should be selection of students for transfer to the different courses" (National Planning Committee, 1948,

tributed to the acceptance of the concept of planning by encouraging departmental and provincial plans for post-war reconstruction, of which the educational plan of the CABE is an example.[20] In 1946 the Advisory Planning Board was constituted to survey the progress which had already been made in the preparation of development plans and to make recommendations for the improvement of planning procedures; one of its recommendations called for the establishment of a national planning body.[21]

It was not necessary, of course, to have a national planning commission before national educational planning could be undertaken—as the existence of the CABE Plan and the Kher Committee Report demonstrates. All that was required were the appropriate formal procedures; a central body with authority to coordinate the views of the states and the Union and to transmit the resulting plan to the states and the central government for implementation would have been sufficient. The CABE and the Union Ministry of Education were both capable of performing these functions with respect to the educational system. But the establishment of the Planning Commission gave India an institution through which the nation's planning procedures could be made more systematic. Since a comprehensive national development plan would have to embrace several sectors of the nation's economic and social life, the Planning Commission was set up and given the responsibility of guiding and coordinating the planning activities of the central ministries and the state governments and of producing the national plan document. The central ministries and states would not abdicate their planning functions, but through the influence of the Planning Commission the various parts of the total plan would be prepared with a greater awareness of their interrelationships.[22] The educational sector (general education) occupies a chapter in each of the three national five-year plans that were produced between 1951 and 1961.

---

pp. 55–56). In this recommendation for limited access to secondary schooling, the committee was in agreement with the CABE Plan and the Kher Committee Report.

[20] See V. T. Krishnamachari (1962, pp. 36–40).

[21] *Ibid.*, pp. 40–43. It is interesting to note that in discussing the priorities to be accorded the development of various sectors of the economy, the Board observed that each sector will "require in a greater or lesser degree an increase in the supply of trained personnel and for the present this may be regarded as Priority No. 1." *Report of the Advisory Planning Board, December, 1946* (Delhi: Manager of Publications, 1947), p. 5. This recognition of the role of education in national development by a non-educational agency parallels the attention given to this relationship by the CABE at an even earlier date (see above, p. 59, footnote 4).

[22] For an authoritative description of the procedures of the Planning Commission, see Krishnamachari (1962). See also A. H. Hanson (1966).

The statement of the Planning Commission's conception of the function of education in a developing society given in the First Five-Year Plan is very similar to that expressed in the CABE Plan. "Education is of basic importance in the planned development of a nation," the Commission asserted. The schools were seen as the means for preparing the appropriate numbers of persons for their occupational roles:

> The educational machinery will have to be geared for the specific tasks which the nation sets itself through the Plan so as to make available in the various fields personnel of suitable quality at the required rate.

But the Planning Commission realized—as had the CABE—that the behavior of persons in their roles as citizens was also involved in the achievement of national development. It stressed, therefore, the need for education in bringing about "intelligent participation of the masses" in the processes of democratic government and "the growth of the spirit of cooperation and . . . disciplined citizenship among the people." Still another aspect of national development to which education could contribute was that of individual development. The schools, the Planning Commission maintained, "should stimulate the growth of the creative faculties, increase the capacity for enjoyment, and develop a spirit of critical appreciation of arts, literature and other creative activities." [23]

For the attainment of these objectives, universal primary schooling would presumably have been an important requirement. Indeed, the Planning Commission emphasized that "the provision of a certain minimum of education to all citizens within a reasonably short period of time is an essential prerequisite, next only to food, for the successful implementation of development programmes and survival of democracy in India." [24] With such a firm conviction in the benefits of primary education, it might be expected that the First Five-Year Plan would have first placed particular stress on the growth of the primary level, as the Kher Commission had done only a year or two earlier.

[23] India, Planning Commission, *The First Five Year Plan* (1952), p. 525. The draft outline of the First Five-Year Plan for the period April, 1951, to March, 1956, was not completed until July, 1951. The draft consisted of two parts, the first relating largely to projects already being executed and the second to those projects which were to be undertaken if external assistance was received. After receiving comments on the plan, a final version was presented in December, 1952, bringing together the various programs into a single plan. *Ibid.*, p. 2.

[24] *Ibid.*, p. 530.

Yet, in spite of the Planning Commission's insistence that "the paucity of our immediate resources makes it imperative that our programmes be selected according to a careful system of priorities, so that the most urgent needs may be met and the most effective use made of the money spent," [25] the rate of expansion proposed for primary schooling was to be the same as that recommended for secondary education.

The Planning Commission proposed that the enrollment ratio for the 6 to 10 age group be increased from approximately 40 percent in 1951 to 60 percent in 1956—a rate of growth which would result in the attainment of universal primary schooling in not much more than the ten years advocated by the Kher Committee. (For purposes of comparison the enrollment ratio targets of this plan and the following five-year plans are given in Table 19.) On the other hand, the limitation imposed in the original Kher Committee plan on the growth of secondary education was no longer considered appropriate. The Planning Commission was satisfied with the existing proportion of students enrolled in secondary education compared to the number of students enrolled in the primary level (about 22 percent) and indicated that this ratio ought to be maintained.[26] If in the five years preceding 1951 primary school enrollments had not increased, no expansion of secondary education should have been required during the period of this plan to preserve the existing ratio between the two levels, because the primary course is of five years' duration, and it would not be until *six* years after the first students entered the new primary schools that they would be ready for secondary schooling. The Planning Commission recognized this relationship, stating that the considerable increase proposed for primary education in the First Five-Year Plan would

> . . . necessitate a corresponding increase in secondary education during the *next* stage of our development, though some expansion would be inevitably required even during the present period to cope with the increased demand for teachers for the large number

[25] *Ibid.*

[26] *Ibid.*, pp. 525–526, 531. No ratio is actually given in the plan; however, in 1951 total enrollment in grades VI–XI was approximately 4,300,000 compared to 19,150,000 in grades I–V. The computed ratio of 22 percent is to be distinguished from the figure of 20 percent which the CABE and the Kher Committee stated would constitute the number of students completing grade V who should be permitted to enter the high schools (secondary level). Owing to the wastage of students in the school system, a ratio of 22 percent between the total enrollments of the two levels really meant that about 80 percent of the students finishing grade V would pass on to the next level (see the discussion of transition rates, above, pp. 31–34).

TABLE 19
India, Enrollment Ratio Targets of the Five-Year Plans

Year	I–V	VI–VIII	IX–XI
		Grades	
	Enrollment Ratio		
1951 base [a]	40.0	10.0 [b]	10.0 [b]
1956 target [a]	60.0	15.0 [b]	15.0 [b]
1956 base [c]	51.0	19.2	9.4
1961 target [c]	62.7	22.5	11.7
1961 base [d]	63.0	22.6	11.4
1966 target [d]	91.7	30.0	15.6
1961 base [e]	61.1	22.8	11.5
1966 target [e]	76.4	28.6	15.6
1961 base [f]	62.7	24.0	11.7
1966 target [f]	78.1	32.1	16.7
	Percentage Increase		
1951–56 [a]	50	50	50
1956–61 [c]	23	17	24
1961–66 [d]	46	33	37
1961–66 [e]	25	25	36
1961–66 [f]	25	34	43

[a] First Five-Year Plan.
[b] Combined figure for both middle and high school levels.
[c] Second Five-Year Plan.
[d] Draft Third Five-Year Plan.
[e] Third Five-Year Plan.
[f] Revised Third Five-Year Plan.

of schools at the primary stage [level] that would come into being.[27]

Since the enrollment increase necessary to provide additional primary school teachers would have been relatively small,[28] the observa-

[27] *Ibid.*, p. 526. (Emphasis supplied.) In actual fact some increase in primary school enrollment had no doubt taken place in the five years prior to 1951, but the statistics are unavailable. This increase was not considered in the plan, however.

[28] The secondary level enrollment ratio would have had to increase by about 14 percent. This estimate is based on the following calculation: The enrollment in grades I–V in 1951 was 19,150,000. To increase this enrollment in five years

tion of the Planning Commission that in the field of secondary education "the general problem is one of consolidation rather than expansion" would appear to be an accurate statement of its objective in
this plan. However, the actual enrollment ratio adopted in the First
Five-Year Plan as the target for secondary education was, inexplicably,
inconsistent with this stated goal. "At the secondary stage [level],"
the Planning Commission declared, "the target should be to bring 15
percent of the children of the relevant age-group into educational
institutions." [29] Since the 1951 enrollment ratio was given as between
10 and 11 percent, this represented a rate of expansion for secondary
education equivalent to that which had been proposed for the primary
level (about 50 percent).[30]

In its proposals for higher education, however, the Planning Commission seemed to adhere more closely to the recommendations of the
previous plans. "At the post-secondary stage [level]," the Planning
Commission stipulated, "there should be greater adjustment between
the needs of the country and the output of educational institutions."
The school system was, it believed—repeating the words used in the
CABE's plan—"top-heavy." Because the provision of university education was "larger than the base structure can profitably support," the
Planning Commission did not advocate any enrollment increases at
this level except in certain specialized professional fields: "No targets
have been laid down for university education as the problem here is
mostly one of consolidation rather than expansion." Also, in contrast
with its failure to endorse a selective system of secondary education,
the Planning Commission recommended the adoption of a procedure
for selective admission to the universities: "We must develop and
apply selective tests on a large scale so that nobody is allowed to go
up for higher education who is not fit to profit by it." [31]

---

by 50 percent would, with a teacher-pupil ratio of 1:30, require 320,000 new
teachers, or 64,000 per year. Allowing for wastage, the output of secondary
school graduates from a total enrollment of 4,300,000 may be estimated at about
450,000 per year. To increase this number by 64,000 per year would require a
14 percent increase in total enrollment. Assuming population increase to have
the same effect on both the primary and secondary levels, the secondary enrollment ratio would thus also need to increase by 14 percent. This calculation
ignores many of the realities of the Indian situation, such as the problem of educated unemployment (which would mean that the number of new secondary
school graduates actually required could be considerably less) and the question
of whether primary school teachers would need to be matriculates.

[29] *Ibid.*, p. 531.

[30] The plan gave 40.0 percent and 44.5 percent as figures for the 1951 primary level enrollment ratio (*ibid.*, pp. 525, 567) and 10.0 percent 10.8 percent,
and "roughly 11 percent" as the secondary level enrollment ratios (*ibid.*, pp. 526,
567, 531).

[31] *Ibid.*, pp. 526, 528, 532, 540.

In its proposals for secondary education, therefore, the First Five-Year Plan represented a significant departure from the plans that had been prepared by the CABE and the Kher Committee. Whereas the earlier plans were written with a firm conviction of what needed to be done to improve Indian education, the Planning Commission seemed unwilling to establish a specific target for secondary education that was consistent with the logic of its analysis. This is a problem which would become increasingly evident in succeeding educational plans.

The Second Five-Year Plan

The Second Five-Year Plan (1956–1961) continued to emphasize the contribution of education to economic and social development. "The system of education," the Planning Commission stated, "has a determining influence on the rate at which economic progress is achieved." Education, according to the Commission, was also important for its role in fostering the values and attitudes necessary for national development, making possible "widespread participation of the people in all activities and constructive leadership at various levels." [32]

In a general statement of the plan's educational objectives, the Planning Commission declared that it provided for an "expansion of elementary education," a "diversification of secondary education," and an "improvement of standards of college and university education." [33] From this it might be inferred that most if not all growth would take place at the primary level, but the targets established for middle and high school education belie such an assumption. The enrollment ratio at the primary level would be increased by 23 percent, at the middle school level by 17 percent, and at the high school level by 24 percent (Table 19; for purposes of comparison the enrollment targets of this and succeeding five-year plans are shown in Table 20).[34] The enrollment targets of a revised version of the Second Five-Year Plan [35] are given in Table 20; state targets for this plan are presented in Table 21. These revised targets do not alter the basic conclusion that a gen-

[32] India, Planning Commission, *Second Five Year Plan* (1956), p. 500.
[33] *Ibid.*
[34] Only enrollment ratio targets were given in the First Five-Year Plan; enrollment targets, however, were also included in the succeeding five-year plans.
[35] Data provided by S. N. Saraf, Assistant Chief, Education Division, Planning Commission, in a letter dated December 26, 1962.

TABLE 20

India, Enrollment Targets of the Five-Year Plans [a]

Year	I–V	VI–VIII	IX–XI	University
	Enrollment (in Thousands)			
1956 base [b]	24,812	5,095	2,303	720
1961 target [b]	32,540	6,387	3,070	—
1956 base [c]	25,115	4,290	1,952	—
1961 target [c]	31,456	5,361	2,507	—
1961 base [d]	33,000	7,000	2,999	900 [e]
1966 target [d]	53,200	10,500	4,500	1,300 [e]
1961 base [f]	34,340	6,290	2,910	900 [e]
1966 target [f]	49,640	9,750	4,560	1,300 [e]
1961 base [g]	35,234	6,626	2,947	—
1966 target [g]	50,598	10,950	4,911	—
	Percentage Increase			
1956–61 [b]	31	25	33	—
1956–61 [c]	25	25	28	—
1961–66 [d]	61	50	50	44
1961–66 [f]	45	55	57	44
1961–66 [g]	44	65	67	—

[a] First Five-Year Plan did not contain enrollment targets.
[b] Second Five-Year Plan.
[c] Revised Second Five-Year Plan.
[d] Draft Third Five-Year Plan.
[e] Arts, science, and commerce students only.
[f] Third Five-Year Plan.
[g] Revised Third Five-Year Plan.

erally equivalent expansion was envisioned at all three levels of the university-preparatory school system.[36]

The enrollment increase recommended for secondary education

---

[36] The increase at the middle and high school levels might have been justified if the decision of the First Five-Year Plan to maintain the 1951 ratio between enrollments at the primary and secondary levels was being adhered to, but secondary schooling had already undergone a greater expansion during 1951–1956 than primary education, and there would thus seem to have been no reason for any additional increase. According to the statistics given in the Second Five-Year Plan, the primary school enrollment ratio had increased by only 22 percent during the first period, but enrollments at the middle and high school levels had grown by 38 and 47 percent, respectively. India, Planning Commission, *Second Five-Year Plan,* p. 501.

TABLE 21

States, Enrollment Targets, Revised Second Five-Year Plan [a]

State	Grades I–V			Grades VI–VIII			Grades IX–XI		
	1956 Enrollment	1961 Target	Percent of Increase	1956 Enrollment	1961 Target	Percent of Increase	1956 Enrollment	1961 Target	Percent of Increase
Andhra Pradesh	2,359	2,751	17	309	413	34	181	216	19
Assam	815	994	22	146	186	27	68	80	18
Bihar	1,781	2,820	58	277	462	67	144	260	81
Gujarat	1,502	1,748	16	220	248	13	97	112	15
Jammu and Kashmir	126	226	79	33	45	36	15	25	67
Kerala	1,973	2,020	2	381	423	11	155	189	22
Madhya Pradesh	1,400	1,851	32	169	219	30	50	79	58
Madras	2,574	3,174	23	466	570	22	194	212	9
Maharashtra	2,929	3,422	17	443	498	12	193	222	15
Mysore	1,578	2,062	31	247	355	44	129	157	22
Orissa	651	886	36	72	96	33	31	55	77
Punjab	1,225	1,495	22	307	447	46	125	138	10
Rajasthan	537	755	41	107	134	25	45	70	56
Uttar Pradesh	2,805	3,805	36	636	730	15	318	418	31
West Bengal	2,457	2,848	16	378	407	8	172	193	12

[a] Enrollments given in thousands.

clearly contradicted the conclusions reached by the Planning Commission in its analysis of the problems of this level. The Planning Commission acknowledged the plight of unemployed matriculates, which pointed to an over-expansion in the existing system of secondary schools. "Partly because of the 'unilinear' character of secondary education in the past," the Planning Commission affirmed, "the problem of unemployment has been accentuated among matriculates." [37] The Planning Commission reported the findings of the Study Group on Educated Unemployed and suggested that its recommendations for schemes to provide additional employment be implemented on a pilot basis. The Planning Commission observed, however, that "the problem of educated unemployed calls for long-term measures" and warned that the expansion of educational facilities should be "closely linked to the future requirements of the economy and the growth of educational facilities in directions which may accentuate further the problem of educated unemployed should be avoided." [38] Nevertheless, the second plan did not restrict the further growth of enrollment in general secondary schools. In fact, the plan called for the establishment of 1,525 new high/higher secondary schools (an increase of about 14 percent), which would, of course, provide essentially academic training. The 937 multi-purpose high schools that were to be founded during the plan period would similarly merely add to the number of students eligible for university admission. Only in the establishment of junior technical schools, which would "enable students to enter an occupation at the end of the secondary course as semi-skilled workers" or to set up their own businesses, did the plan provide for a form of secondary schooling that would be predominately vocational in character and presumably not afford access to the universities. But the number of junior technical schools required was placed at ninety only. The Planning Commission's hope that "the introduction of diversified courses at the secondary level may succeed to some extent in checking the rush of students to Arts colleges" [39] would thus seem to have been optimistic at best.

As was true of the First Five-Year Plan, the second did not establish any targets for university education. The Planning Commission felt that higher education should "fit more closely into plans of economic and social development," but did not make any specific recommendations regarding enrollment in the arts and science courses.[40]

The Second Five-Year Plan, therefore, did not make up for the

[37] *Ibid.*, p. 509.
[38] *Ibid.*, pp. 123–124.
[39] *Ibid.*, pp. 510, 512.
[40] *Ibid.*, p. 512.

deficiencies of the first plan. It continued to express verbal goals that were satisfactory, but the actual enrollment targets failed to conform with those objectives. In most respects the second plan was strikingly like the first, in spite of the lessons which no doubt had been learned from the country's experience in attempting to implement the previous plan.

The Draft Third Five-Year Plan for Education

Before turning to an exmination of the five-year plan for 1961–1966, it will be useful to examine the draft version of this plan. Much longer than the chapter contained in the final plan (259 pages compared to 33 pages), the Draft Third Five-Year Plan for Education was prepared by the Working Group on Education set up by the Ministry of Education in March, 1959, in response to a directive from the Planning Commission.[41] The Working Group consisted of sixteen members, most of whom were from the Ministry of Education or the Planning Commission. Only one member was from a state education department, but a joint meeting with education secretaries of the state governments was held before the draft was completed.

The Working Group was firmly convinced of the importance of education for national development. "So far as the Education Plan is concerned," the Working Group declared, "it starts with the basic assumption . . . that man is eventually more important than machines, and, therefore, 'investment in man' more important than investment in any material projects." As had been the case in the earlier plans, education was regarded as the essential prerequisite for obtaining effective performances in the diverse roles of a modern society. Primary schooling was called "the sure foundation for all progress and prosperity." At the secondary level, the Working Group recommended "a close relationship between education and occupational needs." [42]

[41] The function of working groups in the preparation of the national five-year plan has been described by S. R. Sen (1961, 226–227). "To make the best possible use of the technical knowledge and experience available in the Ministries," Sen writes, "many of whom have also set up planning cells of their own, the Planning Commission has found it advantageous to set up a number of working groups, comprising selected administrators, economists and technicians from the various Central Ministries and Divisions of the Planning Commission, as a means of co-ordinating the work of the Ministries with its own in formulating plans for different sectors. . . . The system of appointing a number of working groups at the stage of the formulation of a plan is a very important part of the Indian planning procedure [which] ensures that those who will implement the plan will . . . have a sense of participation in the formulation of the plan."

[42] India, Ministry of Education, *Draft Third Five Year Plan for Education* (1960), pp. 3, 12, 29.

The Working Group gave explicit attention to the selection of priorities for educational development. In planning, the Working Group pointed out,

> . . . our first and most pressing problem is—as it has always been —the problem of *priorities*. . . . We have wrestled with this problem during these two [previous five-year] Plans and . . . it may be said that we have adopted a programme of expansion for the primary stage [level] while the emphasis in other stages of education . . . is primarily on the improvement of quality. . . . While it is neither right nor feasible to arrest expansion at these stages—to some extent, it is inevitable and follows from the pressure of the objective situation—our main endeavour is to ensure that the *quality* of education is gradually improved.

Although incorrect in its assessment of the targets that had actually been established in the earlier plans and qualified by the revelation that it was not "feasible" to limit the expansion of post-primary education, this statement seemed to indicate that a relatively greater expansion of primary schooling in comparison with the two higher levels would be recommended. Indeed, the Working Group declared that "the provision of universal education should have top priority." [43] The specific targets established in the plan, however, once again reflected a rather different set of priorities.

At the primary level, no less than universal schooling for the 6 to 10 age group was the avowed goal. Since the need for introducing universal compulsory primary education had "been considered at the highest level and recognized and there is agreement that it should be put through," the Working Group proposed that the enrollment ratio at the primary level should be increased to 91.7 percent by 1966, the end of the plan period. Allowing for wastage, this was the best enrollment ratio that the Working Group felt could be achieved and represented an increase of 46 percent over the enrollment ratio expected in 1961. [44]

In discussing its objectives for the secondary level, the Working Group strongly reiterated its stress on quality instead of quantity, although the Group admitted that, in effect, it was difficult to advocate a halt in the growth of secondary schooling in the face of popular demand. "The emphasis in this field [secondary education] is definitely on consolidation and improvement of the existing position and raising of standards rather than expansion." As a consequence, the

[43] *Ibid.*, pp. 6–7, 29.
[44] *Ibid.*, pp. 27, 31–32.

Working Group stated, "a comparatively modest provision has been made for the opening of new secondary schools." [45] But where previous plans had implied that the development of all levels of the educational system was under the control of the planners, the Working Group now referred to the "irresistible claims of expansion" and "the well-known and persistent public demand for the opening of high schools even in rural and sparesely [sic] populated areas which cannot be denied for any great length of time." [46]

Thus, notwithstanding its stipulation that secondary education would be increased only "modestly," the Working Group postulated a 33 percent increase in the enrollment ratios for the middle school level and a 37 percent expansion of the high school level. These rates of growth closely approach the 46 percent rate indicated for primary schooling, thus appearing to violate the general statement of priorities referred to above (see Table 19; enrollment targets are shown in Table 20). And if, as the Working Group intimated, the targets in secondary education were very likely to be exceeded owing to the efforts of private agencies, the actual rate of growth that could be envisioned would probably equal or even exceed that of the primary level. Therefore, in spite of the existence of a similar contradiction between general statements of purpose and specific goals in the two earlier five year plans, the Working Group had committed the same error in its draft plan; the greater realism which it had displayed in recognizing the pressures for expansion of post-primary education did not succeed in preventing this inconsistency in its planning for the secondary level.

[45] *Ibid.,* pp. 10–11.

[46] *Ibid.,* pp. 54, 63. One of the reasons for the excessive expansion of secondary education in the past, the Working Group pointed out, was the factor of "private enterprise" in the establishment of new schools. "For this reason," the Working Group explained, "in the field of secondary education, the physical achievements have nearly always exceeded the planned targets and to that extent the pace of expansion has been beyond policy control. There is no reason to think that these trends will not persist during the course of our future plans." *Ibid.,* p. 64. Nevertheless, it seems clear that the fundamental factor involved in the over-expansion of secondary education, whether under the aegis of private or public agencies, had been reluctance of the responsible authorities to institute effective controls over this type of education. To attribute to private initiative the responsibility for preventing the achievement of planned targets is to ignore the large contributions which are made out of public funds to the operation of most privately operated secondary schools. Also, to state that the existence of private secondary schools makes it impossible to exercise policy control over the expansion of secondary education fails to take account of the obvious possibilities of establishing lower targets for publicly financed secondary schools in order to compensate for the over-expansion due to private efforts (if such were in fact the case) and, if this measure were inadequate, to institute direct control over privately established secondary schools by withholding recognition.

The same type of inconsistency affected its proposals for the university level, regarding which the Working Group—for the first time since the preparation of the CABE Plan and Kher Committee Report—had specific quantitative recommendations. Echoing the conclusions which had been reached previously in the Second Five-Year Plan (but which had not been reflected in the specific provisions of that plan), the Working Group recognized the waste of scarce resources represented by the training given to the educated unemployed. The "costly incidence" of unemployment among university graduates "may be reduced substantially if admissions to higher education are regulated with reference to the national needs." This position was taken in spite of the admission that "the pressure for extension [of university education] was widespread and persistent." Moreover, its assessment of the problem of educated unemployment was not accompanied by a specific quantitative goal limiting the growth of university enrollments; instead, the Working Group planned for a significant increase. In the draft plan, the figures given show a 1961 enrollment in arts, science, and commerce at the university level of 900,000, which would grow to 1,300,000 in 1966—an increase of 44 percent. Allowing for a planned increase in science enrollment from approximately 270,-000 to 520,000, the enrollments in arts and commerce would therefore expand from 630,000 to 780,000.[47]

The Working Group gave the following reason for not attempting to restrict university enrollment:

> It has been suggested earlier that admissions should be regulated on the basis of adjudged capacity of students to benefit from such education [48] but this would be possible only after the techniques of guidance, examination and selection have been perfected and this alone may take years of planned effort. It will not be realistic to expect that admissions will be regulated right from the start of the Third Plan and allowance will, therefore, have to be made for the normal expected increase.[49]

This argument ignores, however, the fact that medical and engineering colleges in India—faced with extreme pressures for admission —had long been using selection procedures to limit their enrollments.[50] In any event, the Working Group seemed to be saying that the univer-

[47] *Ibid.*, pp. 89, 93, 98–102.

[48] In its prior statement of this suggestion, the Working Group also added the stipulation that such admission should be "consistent with national requirements of manpower." *Ibid.*, pp. 92–93.

[49] *Ibid.*, p. 98.

[50] See K. G. Saiyidain and H. C. Gupta (1962).

sities were incapable of selecting their students—a view with which it is doubtful that the university authorities would have concurred. The weakness of the argument is made even more transparent, however, by the failure of the Working Group to include in the plan any scheme for perfecting the desired selection procedures.

The draft third plan, therefore, continued to reflect the basic shortcoming of the previous five-year plans: a generally excellent verbal assessment of India's educational requirements, but an inability to translate this appraisal into the appropriate specific quantitative objectives. The draft was noteworthy, however, in revealing the opinion of the Working Group that enrollments in post-primary education were, in any case, perhaps not susceptible to planned development.

The Third Five-Year Plan

The general statement presented in this plan on the place of education in national development emphasized, as had similar statements in earlier plans, the multi-faceted impact of the schools on society. If possible, the importance attributed to education was even more forcefully expressed:

> Education is the most important single factor in achieving rapid economic development and technological progress and in creating a social order founded on the values of freedom, social justice and equal opportunity. Programmes of education lie at the base of the effort to forge the bonds of common citizenship, to harness the energies of the people, and to develop the natural and human resources of every part of the country. . . . It is one of the major aims of the Third Plan to expand and intensify the educational effort and to bring every home within its fold, so that from now on, in all branches of national life, education becomes the focal point of planned development.[51]

The basic priorities of the third plan in the field of general education were described as expansion at the primary level and qualitative improvement at the upper levels of the general education system. "The provision of facilities for the education of all children in the age group 6–11 [6–10]," the Planning Commission asserted, would be "the main emphasis" in the plan. At the secondary and university levels the only quantitative objective would be the "extension and improvement of the teaching of science." The Planning Commission admitted that the progress achieved during the previous five-year plans had re-

[51] India, Planning Commission, *Third Five Year Plan* (Delhi: Manager of Publications, 1961), p. 573.

sulted in a proportionately greater expansion of secondary than primary education. "Progress in establishing new schools during the first two Plans was relatively greater in respect of middle and high schools than in the case of primary schools." The establishment during the course of the third plan of educational facilities for "the entire population in the age group 6–11 [6–10]," it felt, would correct this trend to a considerable extent.[52]

When it came to setting the actual targets for primary education, however, the Planning Commission deviated from its expressed intention of providing universal schooling. Because of certain difficulties, such as those of obtaining the requisite number of teachers and persuading parents to keep their children in school, the Planning Commission estimated that by the end of the third plan only 76.4 percent of the age group 6–10 would be enrolled in school, giving a rate of growth of 25 percent. At the secondary level, an increase of 25 percent was projected for the middle school enrollment ratio and one of 36 percent for the high school level, notwithstanding the Planning Commission's expressed intention that secondary education would undergo mainly a qualitative improvement (see Tables 19 and 20). The enrollment ratio and enrollment targets for the states are given in Tables 22 and 23, respectively. These tables reveal that nearly all of the states contemplated an expansion of the middle and high school levels that was as great or greater than the growth envisioned for the primary level, thus showing that the national priorities accurately reflected the situation in the states and were not the result of grossly deviant planning in a few states, which, when combined with the planning of the other states, would make the national priorities appear to be inappropriate. The targets of a revised Third Five-Year Plan [53] are also given in Tables 19 and 20; these figures indicate a greater relative emphasis on the expansion of the high and middle school levels compared to the primary level, with increases in the enrollment ratios projected at 43, 34, and 25 percent respectively.

The problem of educated unemployment was discussed in the third plan, primarily in reference to secondary school graduates. Although it was estimated that the backlog of such unemployment among persons with an "education ranging from the middle courses in schools to the first or second year at college" totalled about one million persons, the Planning Commission did not this time advocate a change in the outputs of the educational system, as it had done in its second plan. Instead, the continued growth of secondary schooling was now accepted. "With the expansion of education at the secondary

[52] *Ibid.*, pp. 573–575.
[53] Data provided in a letter by S. N. Saraf. (See note 35, p. 72.)

TABLE 22

States, Enrollment Ratio Targets, Third Five-Year Plan

State	Grades I–V			Grades VI–VIII			Grades IX–XI		
	1961 Enroll- ment Ratio	1966 Enroll- ment Ratio	Percent of Increase	1961 Enroll- ment Ratio	1966 Enroll- ment Ratio	Percent of Increase	1961 Enroll- ment Ratio	1966 Enroll- ment Ratio	Percent of Increase
Andhra Pradesh	60.3	84.5	40	15.6	21.9	40	8.8	9.6	9
Assam	61.7	77.4	25	27.4	35.3	29	17.5	22.9	31
Bihar	53.5	72.6	36	19.4	26.7	38	12.4	17.3	40
Gujarat	72.0	84.2	17	26.8	34.9	30	12.2	15.9	30
Jammu and Kashmir	45.0	62.3	38	27.8	33.5	21	9.9	11.8	19
Kerala	108.8	108.7	−0.1	50.3	45.4	−10	21.6	24.2	12
Madhya Pradesh	47.0	64.0	36	16.3	20.3	25	4.3	5.3	23
Madras	78.9	100.0	27	30.1	35.9	19	13.4	17.3	29
Maharashtra	73.3	90.5	23	28.5	36.2	27	13.6	18.2	34
Mysore	67.4	88.2	31	23.8	29.5	24	10.4	12.3	18
Orissa	47.8	64.6	35	7.9	13.1	66	4.2	7.4	76
Punjab	61.8	74.6	21	28.3	33.8	19	12.0	16.1	34
Rajasthan	42.0	68.2	62	14.8	23.9	61	7.4	11.2	51
Uttar Pradesh	45.4	61.7	36	18.6	20.5	10	12.2	15.3	25
West Bengal	65.6	73.4	12	21.1	33.3	58	11.2	21.9	96

TABLE 23

States, Enrollment Targets, Third Five-Year Plan [a]

State	Grades I–V			Grades VI–VIII			Grades IX–XI		
	1961 Enrollment	1966 Enrollment	Percent of Increase	1961 Enrollment	1966 Enrollment	Percent of Increase	1961 Enrollment	1966 Enrollment	Percent of Increase
Andhra Pradesh	2,820	4,420	57	355	613	73	186	236	27
Assam	1,068	1,508	41	205	325	59	110	171	55
Bihar	3,200	4,800	50	550	925	68	310	500	61
Gujarat	2,000	2,663	33	356	577	62	148	226	53
Jammu and Kashmir	197	302	53	60	88	47	20	27	35
Kerala	2,344	2,661	14	544	619	14	225	295	31
Madhya Pradesh	2,000	3,000	50	327	496	52	78	110	41
Madras	3,350	4,750	42	636	936	47	266	397	49
Maharashtra	3,900	5,400	38	725	1,147	58	315	497	58
Mysore	2,144	3,144	47	364	564	55	147	205	39
Orissa	1,000	1,600	60	85	170	100	40	80	100
Punjab	1,686	2,286	36	375	555	48	145	225	55
Rajasthan	1,151	2,100	82	191	385	102	86	153	78
Uttar Pradesh	4,043	6,650	64	860	1,160	35	512	740	45
West Bengal	2,852	3,502	23	472	902	91	238	530	123

[a] Enrollments given in thousands.

level, greater attention should be given to the absorption of educated persons into gainful employment." [54] This statement was as close as the third plan would come to the more explicit admission of the draft plan that the continued expansion of secondary education was apparently inevitable.

The third plan did not even mention the fact that university graduates were also numbered among the educated unemployed. In fact, the treatment of the requirements for university education in the plan—with its frequent references to the programs and activities of the University Grants Commission—seemed to suggest a relinquishment of responsibility for the planning of this level to the Commission, which had already been described in the draft third plan as "the highest organ for developing the entire field of higher education in the country." [55] The projection for 1966 university enrollments in arts, science and commerce courses was 1,300,000, compared to an estimated enrollment of 900,000 in 1961.[56] These are the same figures that were presented in the draft plan.

Assessment of Educational Planning Goals

Having analyzed separately India's Third Five-Year Plan and each of its predecessors, it will now be useful to consider these plans jointly and to evaluate the efforts of the planners in determining appropriate goals for the country's educational development. Each plan, with the exception of the Kher Committee Report (which is in some ways a supplement to the CABE Plan), contains a general statement of the function of education in the achievement of national development. All of these statements take the view that education is essential for achieving some of the behaviors required in various social roles, such as worker, modern citizen, and leader of society. The significance of this view lies in its implicit acceptance of the concept of role performance as the basis for the determination of national educational requirements, as described in Chapter III.

All of the plans contain a verbal statement of the developmental priorities which should prevail during the plan period. Only in the CABE Plan is a uniform rate of expansion of the three principal educational levels considered desirable; in each of the other plans expansion of the primary level with little or no increase of post-primary schooling is advocated (with the exception of the First Five-Year Plan,

---

[54] India, Planning Commission, *Third Five Year Plan*, pp. 166–167.
[55] India, Planning Commission, *Draft Third Five Year Plan for Education*, p. 89.
[56] India, Planning Commission, *Third Five Year Plan*, p. 576.

in which this order of priorities is somewhat qualified with respect to the secondary level). This prevailing conception of the necessary priorities is usually supported by reference to the social imperative for universal primary schooling and the problem of educated unemployment, again in keeping with the conclusions reached in Chapter III.

Each of the plans also presents its quantitative targets for educational development. It is through the establishment of these specific objectives that precise meaning is presumably given to the order of priorities expressed verbally in the plans. However, in all of the plans except those of the CABE and the Kher Committee, the priorities implicit in the specific quantitative objectives established for the plans differ significantly from the order of priorities given verbally in the plans. Instead of expanding primary schooling relative to the secondary level, the reverse order of priority is actually indicated in the third of the five-year plans, while the first postulates a uniform rate of development, and the second plan and the draft third plan, a rate that is nearly so.

India's five-year plans have thus afforded at best an equivocal guide for the nation's educational development. If the verbal statements of priorities given in the plans were followed, development could have taken place along optimal lines. But if instead, the specific quantitative targets were adhered to, the plans would have a dysfunctional effect. In order to ascertain the consequences of planning for the growth of the school system, it will now be necessary to examine the actual course of India's quantitative educational development during the post-independence period.

V   *Educational Planning:*
Implementation

The principal task of this chapter is to delineate India's quantitative educational development during the period 1950–1961. From these data it will be possible to determine the extent to which the quantitative targets of the five-year plans have been achieved and, by comparing relative rates of growth, to ascertain whether the order of priority involved in this expansion has corresponded either to the verbal statements of priorities suggested in the educational plans or to those priorities entailed in the specific quantitative objectives of these plans.

Some method of measuring educational development is required for these assessments. It will be necessary, of course, to apply the two measures used in the plans to indicate educational targets: the total enrollments and the enrollment ratios of each level of the school system. However, as these measures are not entirely satisfactory, additional indices of educational development involving enrollments in single grades and outputs from the school system will also be employed.

Growth of the School System, 1950-1961

The use of total enrollment statistics for each educational level affords the most convenient method of ascertaining the attainment or non-attainment of plan objectives. Certain enrollment targets are projected in the plans; a comparison of these targets with the actual achievement at the end of the plan period reveals whether any shortfall or over-achievement has taken place. Before turning to this assessment, however, the basic sources for Indian educational statistics need to be identified and some of their characteristics briefly discussed. The major source is the national Ministry of Education, which collects statistics from the states and prepares two annual reports in which detailed statistics are provided: *Education in the States* and *Education in India.* These reports cover all three levels of the school system; in addition, the Ministry publishes an annual statistical report confined to the university level entitled *Education in Universities in India*. Statistics for universities are also available in various statistical reports produced by the University Grants Commission. Most if not all of the state governments publish statistical reports, but these generally appear several years later than the national reports for the same year (which themselves may be three or four years late). In the present investigation, unpublished data from the Ministry of Education for the year 1961 and some earlier years were also utilized,[1] as well as certain data obtained from state educational departments. The enrollment statistics presented in the tables to follow are those of March 31 of the particular year concerned; this date is taken as the date for the termination of the academic year, which is considered to begin on April 1 of the preceding calendar year.[2] Examination results pertain to students educated during the academic year. All figures refer to recognized educational institutions,[3] which comprise the vast majority of schools. These statistics of the Indian educational system are regarded as generally reliable; in any case, they constitute the data used by the educational planners for the determination of present capabilities and future requirements, and thus would seem to provide the appropriate basis for evaluating the success of Indian educational planning.

The growth of total enrollments in the three levels of the university-preparatory school system during 1950–1961 is shown in Table 24.[4] Comparing these data with those given in Table 20, it is evident that all of the enrollment targets of the Second Five-Year Plan (enrollment targets were not given in the first plan) except for the high school level (grades IX–XI) were achieved by 1961; all of the targets of the Revised Second Five-Year Plan were attained by that date without exception. However, because the base year enrollment figures used in the plans do not coincide with the more accurate statistics

[1] Provided in a letter from Gurbax Singh, Assistant Educational Adviser, Ministry of Education, May 27, 1963.

[2] The five-year plan periods also commence on April 1 and terminate on March 31, the dates which delimit the fiscal year.

[3] Recognized institutions are defined as "those in which the course of study followed is that prescribed or recognized by the Government or by a University or by a Board of Secondary and Intermediate Education constituted by law and which satisfy one or more of these authorities, as the case may be, that they attain to a reasonable standard of efficiency. They are open to inspection and their pupils are ordinarily eligible for admission to public examinations and tests held by the Government or the University or the Board." India, Ministry of Education, *Education in India: 1957–58*, II (Delhi: Manager of Publications, 1962), p. 11.

[4] Owing to the continued existence of autonomous princely states within the present territory of India for some time after independence in 1947, it is not possible to obtain statistics for the entire country for an earlier year than 1950.

TABLE 24

India, Enrollments of Educational Levels, 1950–1961

Year	Sex	Primary (Grades I–V)	Middle (Grades VI–VIII)	High School (Grades IX–X)	High School (Grades IX–XI)	University (Total)	University (Arts and Science)
		Enrollment (in Thousands)					
1950	MF [a]	18,193	2,844	846	1,045	383	299
	M [b]	13,060	2,376	733	905	342	263
1951	MF	19,154	3,120	958	1,180	423	326
	M	13,770	2,586	828	1,019	377	285
1956	MF	25,167	4,293	1,517	1,857	736	575
	M	17,528	3,426	1,263	1,540	640	491
1961	MF	34,936	6,699	2,325	2,838	1,084 [c]	800 [c]
	M	23,558	5,070	1,883	2,303	904 [c]	652 [c]
		Percentage Increase					
1951– 56	MF	31	38	58	57	74	76
	M	27	32	53	51	70	72
1956– 61	MF	39	56	53	53	47	39
	M	34	48	49	50	41	33
1950– 61	MF	92	136	175	172	183	168
	M	80	113	157	154	164	148

Educational Level

[a] Males and females.
[b] Males.
[c] 1961 figures partially estimated.

available at a later date, it is necessary to examine the rates of increase for each level in order to determine whether the magnitude of the 1961 achievement corresponds to the intentions of the planners. These data reveal that the rates of increase for all levels of the university-preparatory school system were greater than those envisioned in both versions of the second plan, but the rates of increase for the middle and high school levels exceeded the planned rates by approximately twice the amount by which the rate of increase of the primary level surpassed its target.

The relative rates of growth in total enrollments of the levels of the school system are also indicative of the actual priorities for educational development that existed during the two plan periods. As shown in Table 24, during 1956–1961 the middle and high school levels increased by 56 and 53 percent respectively, and the university level (arts and science) by 39 percent, compared with an increase in primary schooling of 39 percent. The priorities entailed in these achievements contradict both those implied in the verbal statements of requirements contained in the second plan, which indicated a relatively greater expansion of primary education compared to post-primary schooling, and the priorities involved in the quantitative goals that were established, which projected roughly equivalent rates of expansion for the primary and secondary levels. The actual priorities which obtained during 1951–1956 are also difficult to reconcile with the objectives of the plans. Although the first plan did not offer enrollment targets, the verbal statements of priorities and the enrollment ratio targets that were given suggested no more than an equivalent rate of growth for secondary schooling compared to the primary level, with no increase for general university education. Yet the rates of increase during the first plan period were even more unbalanced in favor of the higher levels of the school system than they were in the second period. As a consequence, the rates of growth which were achieved during 1950–1961 show—in relation to the primary level—a much faster rate of increase for the university level (both for total enrollment and enrollment in arts and science), the high school level, and the middle school level: an inversion of the priorities that were contemplated in the verbal statements of the nation's educational plans.

Separate figures are shown in Table 24 (and many of the following tables) for male enrollments. As might be expected, the education of males increased less rapidly than the combined rate for males and females, but the order of priority involved was similar. Data are also given in this table for the rate of growth of enrollment in grades IX–X, which—because some states have only ten years of university-preparatory schooling—might conceivably have differed from the figures for the rate of growth of grades IX–XI; but the rates are essentially uniform.

Table 25 provides additional detailed statistics on the expansion of enrollments at the university level during 1951–1960, based on data from the University Grants Commission. The relatively greater rate of growth of university education during 1951–1956 than during the following four-year period is indicated, as well as the relatively greater progress of the professional faculties compared to the arts, science, and commerce faculties. Nevertheless, as Table 24 shows, general university education, even during the more recent period, has continued to expand at a rate at least equivalent to that of the primary level.

The second method of presenting targets utilized in the five-year plans is in the form of enrollment ratios for each of the educational levels. This measure of educational development is a more satisfactory one than simple enrollment totals, because it takes account of possible variations in the rates of growth in the age groups corresponding to the educational levels, and because an enrollment ratio affords some measure of the extent of schooling being provided. The latter factor is especially significant, of course, where the goal of universal schooling is concerned.

The improvements in enrollment ratios which took place during 1951–1961 are shown in Table 26. Neither the target for the primary level given in the First Five-Year Plan (see Table 19) nor the one for the secondary level was achieved by 1956 (using the data in Table 26, the secondary level enrollment ratio in 1951 may be calculated as 9.2 percent; it rose to only 11.8 percent in 1956, well below the goal of 15 percent). Both the primary and middle school enrollment ratio targets that were established in the Second Five-Year Plan, however, were essentially achieved by the end of the plan period, with only the high school level achievement lagging somewhat behind the target.

Yet because of inadequacies in the statistics used to ascertain enrollment ratios in the base year, the achievement or non-achievement of planned enrollment ratio targets lacks significance for all except the primary level, where reasonably accurate figures were used for both 1951 and 1956. The rates of planned and actual increase in enrollment ratios are, therefore, more meaningful indicators of the attainment of plan goals. The rate of increase of 50 percent projected for the primary and secondary levels during the first plan period was not reached, although it was most closely approached at the high school level and deviated from to the greatest degree at the primary level. During the second plan period, the rate envisioned for the primary level was attained, but the rates for the middle and high school

TABLE 25

India, Enrollments by Faculties in Relation to Total University Enrollment, 1951–1960

Item	1951	1956	Percentage Increase, 1951–56	1960	Percentage Increase, 1956–60	Percentage Increase, 1951–60
Total, university level	396,745	712,697	80	997,137	40	151
Arts faculty	180,806	361,904	100	472,183	30	161
Science faculty	127,168	197,475	55	292,190	48	130
Commerce faculty	34,067	64,167	88	84,127	31	147
Total: arts, science, and commerce faculties	342,041	623,546	82	848,500	36	148
Professional faculties	54,704	89,151	63	148,637	67	172

TABLE 26
India, Enrollment Ratios of Educational Levels, 1951–1961

Year	Enrollment (in Thousands)	Population of Relevant Age Group [a] (in Thousands)	Enrollment Ratio (Percent)	Percentage Increase of Ratio During Preceding Five-Year Period
		Primary Level (Grades I–V)		
1951	19,154	44,473	43.0	—
1956	25,167	50,294	50.0	16
1961	34,936	56,115	62.3	25
		Middle Level (Grades VI–VIII)		
1951	3,120	24,269	12.9	—
1956	4,293	27,022	15.9	23
1961	6,699	29,775	22.5	42
		High School Level (Grades IX–XI)		
1951	1,180	22,580	5.2	—
1956	1,857	24,920	7.5	44
1961	2,838	27,261	10.4	39

[a] Relevant age groups as follows: grades I–V, ages 6–10; grades VI–VIII, ages 11–13; grades IX–XI, ages 14–16.

levels were considerably exceeded. For the period 1951–1961, the following rates of increase may be calculated from Table 26: the primary level enrollment ratio increased by only 45 percent, while the middle level enrollment ratio increased 74 percent and the high school ratio 100 percent. These rates of increase in enrollment ratios, although smaller than those for total enrollments because of the negative effect of population growth, are in proportion to the latter (shown in Table 24). Therefore, the conclusion reached from the analysis of total enrollment figures that the priorities postulated verbally in the plans had actually been reversed during their implementation is also supported by the data for enrollment ratios.

But measures of educational development based on statistics for entire educational levels are inadequate for a school system such as India's in which wastage and stagnation are prevalent factors. It is the output from a given level of the educational system that is the significant indicator of its performance for the society concerned; this figure may change at a rate different from that of the total enrollment of the educational level to which it is related. Table 27, therefore, presents

TABLE 27

India, Outputs and Intakes of the Educational System, 1950–1961

Year	Sex	Grade II Enrollment	Grade V Enrollment	Grade VI Enrollment	Grade VIII Enrollment	Grade X Enrollment	Secondary Level Graduates (Matriculates)c	B.A. Degrees	B.Sc. Degrees
				Totals (in Thousands)					
1950	MF a	4,136	1,733	1,150	719	368	189	19.2	9.5
	M b	2,941	1,344	958	610	320	163	15.3	8.7
1951	MF	4,332	1,898	1,246	851	420	241	21.3	11.0
	M	3,108	1,475	1,015	723	367	211	17.3	10.1
1956	MF	5,523	2,403	1,698	1,160	675	429	38.0	16.0
	M	3,823	1,822	1,337	940	566	357	29.7	14.4
1961	MF	7,502	3,605	2,725	1,756	1,047	662	—	—
	M	5,040	2,585	2,033	1,365	860	527	—	—
				Percentage Increase					
1951–56	MF	27	27	36	36	61	78	78	45
	M	23	24	32	30	54	69	72	4
1956–61	MF	36	50	60	51	55	54	—	—
	M	32	42	52	45	52	48	—	—
1950–61	MF	81	108	137	144	185	250	—	—
	M	71	92	112	124	169	223	—	—

a Males and females.
b Males.
c Includes graduates of higher secondary schools.

93

data on the outputs from the various educational levels during 1950–1961. Since reliable figures on the numbers of graduates from the primary and middle levels are not available, total enrollment figures for grades V and VIII have been substituted on the assumption that the numbers of students completing the two levels are proportional to the enrollments in these two grades; data for grade X enrollments (which may be taken to represent the final grade of high school) are also shown to provide a basis for relating the preceding sets of terminal grade enrollment statistics (apparent outputs) to the data on the actual numbers of matriculates and bachelor's degrees.[5] The rates of increase of these measures of output generally show, for 1951–1956 and 1950–1961, the same relative increases revealed in Tables 24, 25, and 26 with respect to total enrollments of the educational levels and their enrollment ratios. However, for the period of the second plan, a somewhat better performance for the primary level in relation to the middle and high school levels is indicated, with the outputs for these three levels increasing at an approximately equivalent rate.

Statistics on the output of matriculates are also useful in determining whether the expansion of secondary schooling was justified on the basis of providing the teachers required for an expansion of primary level enrollments.[6] The increase in these enrollments between 1950–1961 was 16,743,000; at a teacher-pupil ratio of 1:30, approximately 558,000 additional teachers would have been necessary, for an average of about 50,000 per year. This growth in secondary school output was achieved as soon as 1951, however, thus indicating that most of the increase in the output of matriculates which took place during 1950–1961 was not warranted by the teacher requirements of the primary level.

While statistics on the outputs from the various levels of the school system are helpful in assessing the performance of the system, it may be questioned whether such data afford the most desirable basis for measuring the attainment of planned priorities for educational development. As a result of the time lag inherent in the flow of students through the school system, the outputs achieved during a given plan period reflect the inflow of students which began several years earlier, when the priorities of a different plan may have been in effect. Thus, for a more adequate indication of the priorities governing edu-

---

[5] In a strict sense the gradewise enrollments are not those of the final year for the particular levels involved, since the terminal grade of the primary course, for example, is grade IV in some states and grade V in others. Nevertheless, to the extent that an error results, it would probably have a constant effect during the period 1950–1961 and thus would not affect the interpretation of relative rates of development.

[6] See also above, pp. 69–71.

cational development during a particular plan period, it is necessary to analyze the relative rates of increase which took place in the intake of students to the major levels of the school system. In Table 27, these data are represented by the statistics for total enrollments in grades II and VI, which are assumed to have a constant relationship to the actual intake into the primary and secondary levels, respectively.[7] A comparison of the rates of increase of these enrollments shows the same inversion of priorities that was revealed in the analysis of the statistics in Tables 24 and 26. The enrollment data for grades II and VI also indicate the placement of a greater priority on the expansion of secondary education relative to the primary level during 1956–1961, which is not shown in the output statistics for that period.

The relationships shown in Table 27 are also given in Table 28. This table makes use of the enrollment and output statistics contained in Table 27, but presents these data as percentages of the grade V enrollment; in addition, data for enrollment in grade I are included. The decrease in the percentages of grades I and II between 1956–1961 reveals how the relatively better performance of primary school outputs compared to the rate of growth of the total enrollment and enrollment ratio of this level in the same period was achieved. Table 28 also shows the relatively greater apparent retention of males in the school system compared to females. The output of males from the post-primary levels is consistently higher than the combined outputs for males and females in relation to comparable figures for grade V; the situation is reversed, however, in grades I and II.

Table 29 permits a direct appraisal of India's educational development in terms of the quantitative indices presented in Chapter III. The secondary level completion ratio was 3.3 percent in 1951. As the evidence of educated unemployment discussed in Chapter III suggests, this was probably excessive; but it was within the range of 1 to 5 percent postulated for a Stage I educational system. The 5.6 percent ratio for males, however, had already surpassed the upper limit for

---

[7] The enrollment in grade I has not been selected as the measure for the intake to the primary level because the enrollment in this grade probably did not require expansion through at least part of the 1951–1961 period in order to allow 100 percent of the relevant age group to enter the primary level; in 1956, for example, the grade I enrollment ratio was approximately 96 percent, and this increased to 112 percent by 1961. The enrollment in grade II—which, after grade I, is closest to the point of access to the primary level—would, however, have had to expand considerably in nearly every state during 1951–1961: in 1961, the grade II enrollment ratio for the country had reached only 65 percent; it was 114 percent in Kerala, 96 percent in Madras, and 80 percent in Maharashtra, the state with the third highest ratio. The rate of growth in grade II would, therefore, constitute a sensitive indicator of the amount of effort being made to bring about universal primary schooling.

TABLE 28
India, Static Relationships between
Educational Levels, 1950–1961

Item	Sex	Year 1950	1951	1956	1961
Grade I enrollment as percent of grade V enrollment	MF [a]	398	366	414	371
	M [b]	355	323	366	336
Grade II enrollment as percent of grade V enrollment	MF	239	228	230	208
	M	219	211	210	195
Grade V enrollment as percent of itself	MF	100	100	100	100
	M	100	100	100	100
Grade VI enrollment as percent of grade V enrollment	MF	66.4	65.6	70.6	75.6
	M	71.2	68.8	73.4	78.6
Grade VIII enrollment as percent of grade V enrollment	MF	41.5	44.9	48.3	48.7
	M	45.4	49.0	51.6	52.8
Grade X enrollment as percent of grade V enrollment	MF	21.2	22.1	28.1	29.0
	M	23.8	25.0	31.0	33.3
Matriculates as percent of grade V enrollment [c]	MF	10.9	12.7	17.9	18.4
	M	12.2	14.3	19.6	20.4
B.A. degrees as percent of grade V enrollment	MF	1.11	1.12	1.58	—
	M	1.14	1.17	1.63	—
B.Sc. degrees as percent of grade V enrollment	MF	0.55	0.58	0.67	—
	M	0.65	0.68	0.79	—

[a] Males and females.
[b] Males.
[c] Includes graduates of higher secondary schools.

this stage. The grade V enrollment ratio, on the other hand, was only 22.9 percent for the total population and 34.5 percent for males. By the end of the first plan period, although the secondary level output had expanded to 5.3 percent, the grade V ratio had improved only slightly to 26.0 percent, thus requiring the school system to be classified under the heading of Stage II Deviation. During the second plan period the grade V enrollment ratio exhibited a faster rate of in-

TABLE 29

India, Terminal Grade Enrollment Ratios and Secondary Level Completion Ratios, 1951–1961

Year	Sex	Number (in Thousands)	Population of Relevant Age Group [a] (in Thousands)	Enrollment or Completion Ratio	Percentage Increase of Ratio During Preceding Five-Year Period
		Grade V Enrollment			
1951	MF [b]	1,898	8,285	22.9	—
	M [c]	1,475	4,274	34.5	—
1956	MF	2,403	9,256	26.0	14
	M	1,822	4,758	38.3	11
1961	MF	3,605	10,226	35.3	36
	M	2,585	5,241	49.3	29
		Grade X Enrollment			
1951	MF	420	7,525	5.6	—
	M	367	3,895	9.4	—
1956	MF	675	8,304	8.1	45
	M	566	4,287	13.2	40
1961	MF	1,047	9,083	11.5	42
	M	860	4,678	18.4	39
		Secondary Level Graduates (Matriculates) [d]			
1951	MF	241	7,346	3.3	—
	M	211	3,793	5.6	—
1956	MF	429	8,087	5.3	61
	M	357	4,171	8.6	54
1961	MF	662	8,828	7.5	42
	M	527	4,548	11.6	35

[a] Relevant age groups as follows: grade V, age 11; grade X, age 15; secondary level graduates, age 16.

[b] Males and females.

[c] Males.

[d] Includes graduates of higher secondary schools.

crease than it had in the previous period, improving to 35.3 percent in 1961, but the secondary level completion ratio had an even more rapid rate of growth and now stood at 7.5 percent. The output of males from the secondary level at 11.6 percent was very high relative to the grade V enrollment ratio of males of 49.3 percent. By the end of its first two five-year plans, therefore, India was still far from achieving the goal of universal primary schooling, with only one out of every three children of school age reaching grade V. On the other hand, in spite of the relatively large proportion of secondary school graduates being produced in 1951, the output from the secondary level during the following ten years grew even more rapidly than the grade V enrollment ratio, showing once again that the verbal statements of priorities which had been given in the plans were actually reversed during the implementation of the plans.

A fundamental reason for this failure to achieve the required priorities is shown in Table 30. In the absence of effective procedures for restricting access to the higher levels of the school system, there

TABLE 30
India, Progressive Relationships between Educational Levels, 1950–1961

Base Year	Sex	Grade V Enrollment in Base Year as Percent of Itself	Grade VIII Enrollment 3 Years Later as Percent of Grade V Enrollment in Base Year	Grade X Enrollment 5 Years Later as Percent of Grade V Enrollment in Base Year	High School Graduates 6 Years Later as Percent of Grade V Enrollment in Base Year [c]
1950	MF [a]	100	53.7	36.4	24.8
	M [b]	100	57.7	39.7	26.6
1951	MF	100	53.1	35.6	24.6
	M	100	56.5	38.3	26.0
1952	MF	100	53.1	36.6	25.7
	M	100	56.1	39.4	27.4
1953	MF	100	53.5	37.0	24.5
	M	100	56.8	40.3	26.4
1954	MF	100	55.0	38.9	25.9
	M	100	57.5	42.0	26.7
1955	MF	100	57.1	40.6	28.8
	M	100	59.3	44.1	30.1
1956	MF	100	59.9	43.6	—
	M	100	62.0	47.2	—
1957	MF	100	58.2	—	—
	M	100	61.0	—	—
1958	MF	100	64.0	—	—
	M	100	67.5	—	—

[a] Males and females.
[b] Males.
[c] Includes graduates of higher secondary schools.

has been an increasing tendency for those students who apparently complete the primary level to undergo schooling at the higher levels of the educational system. For example, the enrollment in grade VIII in 1953 was only 53.7 percent of the grade V enrollment in 1950; by 1961, however, the grade VIII enrollment had become 64.0 percent of the grade V enrollment three years earlier. Thus, while it is appropriate to compare the relative rates of increase of the different levels or grades of the school system during a particular period of time as evidence of the priorities accorded their development during that period, the rate of increase of one educational level or grade can be compared to another with respect to a possible causal connection only if recognition is taken of the time lag entailed in the normal progression of students from one level to the next. The equivalent rates of increase in output achieved by the primary-, middle-, and high-school levels during 1956–1961 should not be taken to indicate, therefore, that the rates of increase will also be equivalent in the third-plan period. The 1956–1961 increase of middle school outputs was related to the primary level outputs of 1953–1958, while the growth in grade X enrollments during the second plan period was related to primary school outputs in 1951–1956; as Table 30 makes clear, these middle- and high-school outputs increased at a faster rate than the primary school outputs to which they actually correspond.

Educational Development in the States, 1957-1961

An analysis of India's post-independence educational development would not be complete without consideration of the progress that has been made in each of the fifteen major states. Only if most of the states are in the same stage of educational development is it possible to combine the quantitative requirements of the separate states and accurately reflect the needs of the nation.[8] To take a hypothetical example, if half of the states (with half of the population) had already attained universal primary schooling, these states would presumably be attempting to expand post-primary educational enrollments. If the remaining states had only a 10 percent completion ratio at the primary level and adequate development of the higher levels of the school system, these states would presumably be giving principal emphasis to the expansion of primary education. On a national basis these statistics would result in a primary level completion ratio of about 55 percent and a more than sufficient completion ratio at the secondary level,

[8] This proposition is valid only for countries with decentralized responsibility for education; it would not hold for those countries in which the entire nation is regarded as the effective unit for education. See also above, p. 49.

suggesting that the country as a whole ought to withhold further expansion of secondary schooling and concentrate its efforts on the development of the primary level.

Yet, given the hypothetical situations prevailing in the states used for this example, optimal plans for development from the point of view of each state would give rise to what would seem to be inappropriate priorities for the nation as a whole. The states with only 10 percent primary level completion ratios might plan a 100 percent improvement of these ratios by increasing them to 20 percent, but the national figure would increase to about 60 percent, for a growth of approximately 10 percent. In the advanced states, since they would have no requirement to expand primary schooling or even the possibility of doing such, any increase would be in the post-primary levels of the school system. Since this expansion might well be 20 percent or more, the effect would be to show a national set of priorities for educational development in which secondary schooling was expanding as fast or faster than the primary level, contrary to the expected priorities for a Stage II educational system. The possibility of this hypothetical situation resembling the realities of the Indian situation makes it imperative, therefore, to examine the development of each of the state educational systems.

As shown in Tables 17 and 18, by 1961 all of the states except three had achieved secondary level completion ratios in excess of 5 percent, and only one state had attained universal primary schooling. The rates of increase in total enrollments during 1957–1961 that brought about these achievements and those at the middle school and university levels are given in Tables 31 through 34.[9] These rates may be compared with the rates projected during the Revised Second Five-Year Plan (Table 21).[10] While it had been envisioned in the targets of this plan that primary schooling would increase at a faster rate than both levels of secondary education in six states, the actual achievement during 1957–1961 revealed that primary education increased more rapidly than both the middle and high school levels in only three states (Orissa, Rajasthan, and Uttar Pradesh). Primary schooling expanded more rapidly than university education in only four states (Andhra Pradesh, Bihar, Orissa, and Rajasthan).

Tables 35 through 49 provide data on the progress of educational

---

[9] Reliable data for 1956 enrollments are not available, owing to the rearrangement of state boundaries which took place in that year.

[10] The targets specified in the Revised Second Five-Year Plan refer to grades I–V, VI–VIII, and IX–XI, rather than to the levels of the university-preparatory school system as actually defined in the various states; the latter are referred to, however, in Tables 31 through 34.

TABLE 31
States, Primary Level Enrollments, 1957–1961

State	Sex	Enrollments (in Thousands)		
		1957	1961	Percentage Increase
Andhra Pradesh	MF [a]	2,454.1	2,976.1	21.3
	M [b]	1,544.0	1,840.7	19.2
Assam	MF	862.5	1,125.6	30.5
	M	557.0	710.8	27.6
Bihar	MF	1,929.8	3,184.5	65.0
	M	1,574.4	2,445.6	55.3
Gujarat	MF	1,521.5	1,820.6	19.7
	M	998.8	1,161.1	16.2
Jammu and Kashmir	MF	150.2	209.8	39.7
	M	124.0	164.8	32.9
Kerala	MF	1,791.1	2,032.2	13.5
	M	966.7	1,082.6	12.0
Madhya Pradesh	MF	1,536.5	1,995.7	29.9
	M	1,250.7	1,553.8	24.2
Madras	MF	2,609.8	3,333.4	27.7
	M	1,650.9	2,053.1	24.4
Maharashtra	MF	2,852.4	3,533.1	23.9
	M	1,848.8	2,199.7	19.0
Mysore	MF	1,544.6	1,977.3	28.0
	M	965.3	1,229.1	27.3
Orissa	MF	686.9	1,410.9	105.4
	M	514.0	970.9	88.9
Punjab	MF	1,316.8	1,439.7	9.3
	M	941.9	976.7	3.7
Rajasthan	MF	610.4	1,114.5	82.6
	M	507.2	899.0	77.2
Uttar Pradesh	MF	3,002.4	4,096.0	36.4
	M	2,418.1	3,224.8	33.4
West Bengal	MF	2,333.1	2,712.3	16.3
	M	1,538.7	1,701.4	10.6

[a] Males and females.
[b] Males.

development in each of the states, based on enrollments in the initial
and terminal grades of each educational level as actually organized in
the states concerned. These statistics parallel the data for the national
school system given in Table 27. As was the case with the national
figures, the analysis of output and intake data yields a picture of edu-

TABLE 32
States, Middle Level Enrollments, 1957–1961

		Enrollments (in Thousands)		
State	Sex	1957	1961	Percentage Increase
Andhra Pradesh	MF [a]	318.5	407.9	28.1
	M [b]	255.0	315.8	23.8
Assam	MF	160.1	219.9	37.3
	M	121.3	159.1	31.2
Bihar	MF	223.4	390.1	74.6
	M	205.8	345.6	68.0
Gujarat	MF	329.1	501.2	52.3
	M	241.9	352.5	45.7
Jammu and Kashmir	MF	36.5	59.4	62.7
	M	30.4	47.8	57.2
Kerala	MF	622.8	900.7	44.6
	M	356.2	506.5	42.2
Madhya Pradesh	MF	186.7	317.0	69.8
	M	162.1	267.7	65.1
Madras	MF	478.0	690.9	44.5
	M	342.6	481.4	40.5
Maharashtra	MF	667.5	973.1	45.8
	M	505.3	704.2	39.4
Mysore	MF	426.4	554.1	29.9
	M	317.4	394.1	24.2
Orissa	MF	55.7	84.4	51.5
	M	49.4	74.3	50.4
Punjab	MF	327.2	438.6	34.0
	M	269.8	349.7	29.6
Rajasthan	MF	130.6	207.1	58.6
	M	116.6	179.5	53.9
Uttar Pradesh	MF	630.6	826.2	31.0
	M	559.1	703.8	25.9
West Bengal	MF	596.1	767.5	28.8
	M	476.2	564.1	18.5

[a] Males and females.
[b] Males.

cational development that is somewhat different from that obtained from total enrollment statistics. Based on enrollments in the terminal grades (apparent outputs), three states (Mysore, Rajasthan, and West Bengal) had a more rapid rate of growth for primary schooling compared with the post-primary levels of the university-preparatory school

TABLE 33
States, High School Level Enrollments, 1957–1961

State	Sex	Enrollments (in Thousands)		
		1957	1961	Percentage Increase
Andhra Pradesh	MF [a]	175.6	190.7	8.6
	M [b]	152.4	160.0	5.0
Assam	MF	77.4	125.1	61.6
	M	64.2	98.8	53.9
Bihar	MF	241.2	465.8	93.1
	M	229.1	433.9	89.4
Gujarat	MF	155.9	266.0	70.6
	M	123.7	203.0	64.1
Jammu and Kashmir	MF	13.6	22.0	61.8
	M	11.5	16.5	43.5
Kerala	MF	267.7	332.4	24.2
	M	164.5	198.0	20.4
Madhya Pradesh	MF	49.9	94.7	89.8
	M	43.3	80.6	86.1
Madras	MF	203.6	268.6	31.9
	M	159.0	200.9	26.4
Maharashtra	MF	277.4	456.3	64.5
	M	218.2	350.6	60.7
Mysore	MF	90.8	122.8	35.2
	M	72.6	95.3	31.3
Orissa	MF	53.1	67.7	27.5
	M	49.1	61.7	25.7
Punjab	MF	129.5	160.8	24.2
	M	110.2	132.8	20.5
Rajasthan	MF	44.3	69.6	57.1
	M	40.9	63.2	54.5
Uttar Pradesh	MF	284.4	357.5	25.7
	M	261.0	309.5	18.5
West Bengal	MF	153.2	194.1	26.8
	M	125.4	153.3	22.2

[a] Males and females.
[b] Males.

system—the same number as indicated by Tables 31 through 33—but only one of these states (Rajasthan) is identified in both sets of data. The data on the rates of increase in enrollments of grade II and the first grade of the secondary level (apparent intakes) indicate that only three states (Mysore, Orissa, and Uttar Pradesh) were expanding

TABLE 34
States, University Level Enrollments, 1957–1961

		Enrollments		
State	Sex	1957	1961	Percentage Increase
Andhra Pradesh	MF [a]	54,809	57,515	4.9
	M [b]	49,826	50,065	0.5
Assam	MF	15,694	27,811	77.2
	M	13,642	24,165	77.1
Bihar	MF	59,213	93,300	57.6
	M	55,965	86,811	55.1
Gujarat	MF	—	47,482	—
	M	—	38,818	—
Jammu and Kashmir	MF	5,874	8,710	48.3
	M	4,794	6,739	40.6
Kerala	MF	38,300	44,872	17.2
	M	28,630	31,621	10.4
Madhya Pradesh	MF	24,802	47,961	93.4
	M	21,596	41,337	91.4
Madras	MF	51,901	69,671	34.2
	M	44,467	55,284	24.3
Maharashtra	MF	80,173	109,032	36.0
	M	65,462	87,018	32.9
Mysore	MF	40,128	51,431	28.2
	M	34,263	42,963	25.4
Orissa	MF	7,628	14,522	90.4
	M	6,898	12,911	87.2
Punjab	MF	48,311	62,465	29.3
	M	40,196	50,594	25.9
Rajasthan	MF	23,422	32,145	37.2
	M	21,091	28,107	33.3
Uttar Pradesh	MF	186,288	254,590	36.7
	M	167,563	222,645	32.9
West Bengal	MF	119,158	141,072	18.4
	M	98,360	109,249	11.1

[a] Males and females.
[b] Males.

primary schooling more rapidly than the secondary level.[11] This number is identical with that obtained in the two preceding analyses, but

[11] If the comparison were made between grade II and the first grade of the high school level, four states (Andhra Pradesh, Orissa, Rajasthan, and Uttar Pradesh) would show a faster rate of development for the primary level.

TABLE 35
Andhra Pradesh, Educational Development, 1957–1961

| Grade | Sex | Enrollment (in Thousands) | | Percentage Increase, 1957–61 |
		1957	1961	
Grade I	MF [a]	978	1,220	25
	M [b]	588	735	25
Grade II	MF	526	637	21
	M	328	388	18
Last grade of primary level (V)	MF	252	286	13
	M	174	191	10
First grade of middle level (VI)	MF	130	173	33
	M	102	132	29
Last grade of middle level (VIII)	MF	85.1	107	26
	M	70.0	85.1	22
First grade of high school level (IX)	MF	66.9	75.4	13
	M	56.7	62.1	10
Last full grade of high school level (XI)	MF	50.9	54.2	6.4
	M	45.4	46.5	2.4

[a] Males and females.
[b] Males.

TABLE 36
Assam, Educational Development, 1957–1961

| Grade | Sex | Enrollment (in Thousands) | | Percentage Increase, 1957–61 |
		1957	1961	
Grade I	MF [a]	392	508	30
	M [b]	240	309	29
Grade II	MF	159	209	31
	M	104	133	28
Last grade of primary level (V)	MF	78.0	106	36
	M	55.0	71.2	29
First grade of middle level (VI)	MF	59.0	82.8	40
	M	44.0	59.3	35
Last grade of middle level (VIII)	MF	47.5	64.4	36
	M	36.3	46.8	29
First grade of high school level (IX)	MF	24.7	41.0	66
	M	20.2	31.7	57
Last full grade of high school level (XII)	MF	13.9	22.0	58
	M	11.9	18.0	51

[a] Males and females.
[b] Males.

TABLE 37
Bihar, Educational Development, 1957–1961

		Enrollment (in Thousands)		
Grade	Sex	1957	1961	Percentage Increase, 1957–61
Grade I	MF [a]	851	1,471	73
	M [b]	666	1,086	63
Grade II	MF	418	666	59
	M	338	512	51
Last grade of primary level (V)	MF	160	265	66
	M	144	222	54
First grade of middle level (VI)	MF	121	213	76
	M	112	188	68
Last grade of middle level (VII)	MF	102	177	74
	M	94.0	158	68
First grade of high school level (VIII)	MF	76.7	145	89
	M	72.0	133	85
Last full grade of high school level (XI)	MF	42.1	90.6	115
	M	40.5	85.3	111

[a] Males and females.
[b] Males.

TABLE 38
Gujarat, Educational Development, 1957–1961

		Enrollment (in Thousands)		
Grade	Sex	1957	1961	Percentage Increase, 1957–61
Grade I	MF [a]	712	819	15
	M [b]	441	502	14
Grade II	MF	356	411	15
	M	242	265	10
Last grade of primary level (IV)	MF	198	264	33
	M	139	178	28
First grade of middle level (V)	MF	146	210	44
	M	106	146	38
Last grade of middle level (VII)	MF	81.6	131	61
	M	61.0	93.0	52
First grade of high school level (VIII)	MF	55.8	95.5	71
	M	44.3	71.7	62
Last full grade of high school level (XI)	MF	22.1	41.4	87
	M	16.6	32.3	95

[a] Males and females.
[b] Males.

TABLE 39
Jammu and Kashmir, Educational Development, 1957–1961

| | | Enrollment (in Thousands) | | |
| | | | | Percentage Increase, |
Grade	Sex	1957	1961	1957–61
Grade I	MF [a]	49.2	65.3	33
	M [b]	38.2	52.6	38
Grade II	MF	33.8	51.7	53
	M	28.9	38.9	35
Last grade of primary level (V)	MF	20.1	27.4	36
	M	17.1	21.8	27
First grade of middle level (VI)	MF	14.7	22.7	54
	M	12.2	18.2	49
Last grade of middle level (VIII)	MF	10.0	17.5	75
	M	8.39	14.4	72
First grade of high school level (IX)	MF	7.11	12.1	70
	M	5.93	9.81	65
Last full grade of high school level (X)	MF	6.51	9.98	53
	M	5.55	6.70	21

[a] Males and females.
[b] Males.

TABLE 40
Kerala, Educational Development, 1957–1961

| | | Enrollment (in Thousands) | | |
| | | | | Percentage Increase, |
Grade	Sex	1957	1961	1957–61
Grade I	MF [a]	554	613	11
	M [b]	258	321	24
Grade II	MF	479	518	8.1
	M	258	275	6.6
Last grade of primary level (IV)	MF	349	422	21
	M	191	229	20
First grade of middle level (V)	MF	277	359	30
	M	154	198	29
Last grade of middle level (VII)	MF	154	263	71
	M	91.2	150	64
First grade of high school level (VIII)	MF	125	153	22
	M	74.4	90.3	21
Last full grade of high school level (XI/X) [c]	MF	49.9	74.5	49
	M	33.3	45.4	36

[a] Males and females.
[b] Males.
[c] Grade XI in 1957; grade X in 1961.

TABLE 41
Madhya Pradesh, Educational Development, 1957–1961

		Enrollment (in Thousands)		
Grade	Sex	1957	1961	Percentage Increase, 1957–61
Grade I	MF [a]	625	758	21
	M [b]	500	577	15
Grade II	MF	354	434	23
	M	286	335	17
Last grade of primary level (V)	MF	110	197	79
	M	94.0	159	69
First grade of middle level (VI)	MF	77.8	134	72
	M	67.0	112	67
Last grade of middle level (VIII)	MF	46.5	82.9	78
	M	41.0	70.8	73
First grade of high school level (IX)	MF	28.2	49.8	77
	M	24.3	41.9	72
Last full grade of high school level (X)	MF	21.7	44.9	107
	M	19.0	38.6	103

[a] Males and females.
[b] Males.

TABLE 42
Madras, Educational Development, 1957–1961

		Enrollment (in Thousands)		
Grade	Sex	1957	1961	Percentage Increase, 1957–61
Grade I	MF [a]	859	1,065	24
	M [b]	525	631	20
Grade II	MF	611	763	25
	M	384	465	21
Last grade of primary level (V)	MF	294	396	35
	M	197	258	31
First grade of middle level (VI)	MF	196	291	48
	M	139	201	45
Last grade of middle level (VIII)	MF	127	178	40
	M	92.3	125	35
First grade of high school level (IX)	MF	85.2	111	30
	M	65.5	82.0	25
Last full grade of high school level (XI)	MF	50.6	72.8	44
	M	40.4	55.6	38

[a] Males and females.
[b] Males.

TABLE 43
Maharashtra, Educational Development, 1957–1961

| | | Enrollment (in Thousands) | | |
| | | 1957 | 1961 | Percentage Increase, |
Grade	Sex	1957	1961	1957–61
Grade I	MF [a]	1,210	1,489	23
	M [b]	715	864	21
Grade II	MF	714	843	18
	M	477	534	12
Last grade of primary level (IV)	MF	406	538	33
	M	292	365	25
First grade of middle level (V)	MF	283	416	47
	M	212	297	40
Last grade of middle level (VII)	MF	174	244	40
	M	134	179	34
First grade of high school level (VIII)	MF	112	191	71
	M	88.0	145	65
Last full grade of high school level (X)	MF	73.7	116.2	58
	M	58.2	90.3	55

[a] Males and females.
[b] Males.

TABLE 44
Mysore, Educational Development, 1957–1961

| | | Enrollment (in Thousands) | | |
| | | 1957 | 1961 | Percentage Increase, |
Grade	Sex	1957	1961	1957–61
Grade I	MF [a]	719	836	16
	M [b]	420	501	19
Grade II	MF	370	497	34
	M	233	308	32
Last grade of primary level (IV)	MF	200	280	40
	M	139	187	35
First grade of middle level (V)	MF	155	191	23
	M	113	132	17
Last grade of middle level (VII)	MF	93.0	123.1	32
	M	71.1	89.1	25
First grade of high school level (VIII)	MF	66.6	92.5	39
	M	51.3	68.9	34
Last full grade of high school level (X)	MF	40.5	53.8	33
	M	32.6	42.1	29

[a] Males and females.
[b] Males.

TABLE 45
Orissa, Educational Development, 1957–1961

		Enrollment (in Thousands)		
Grade	Sex	1957	1961	Percentage Increase, 1957–61
Grade I	MF [a]	261	701	169
	M [b]	186	450	142
Grade II	MF	167	314	88
	M	122	221	81
Last grade of primary level (V)	MF	44.2	65.5	48
	M	38.0	55.7	47
First grade of middle level (VI)	MF	33.0	46.5	41
	M	29.0	40.6	40
Last grade of middle level (VII)	MF	22.7	37.8	67
	M	20.3	33.7	66
First grade of high school level (VIII)	MF	19.9	23.1	16
	M	18.0	20.9	16
Last full grade of high school level(XII/XI) [c]	MF	6.02	10.4	73
	M	5.51	9.55	73

[a] Males and females.
[b] Males.
[c] Grade XII in 1957; grade XI in 1961.

TABLE 46
Punjab, Educational Development, 1957–1961

		Enrollment (in Thousands)		
Grade	Sex	1957	1961	Percentage Increase, 1957–61
Grade I	MF [a]	441	436	−1.1
	M [b]	301	284	−5.6
Grade II	MF	284	287	1.1
	M	201	193	−4.0
Last grade of primary level (V)	MF	166	215	30
	M	128	157	23
First grade of middle level (VI)	MF	130	178	37
	M	105	140	33
Last grade of middle level (VIII)	MF	84.7	117	38
	M	70.7	94.2	33
First grade of high school level (IX)	MF	75.1	85.2	13
	M	63.9	70.1	10
Last full grade of high school level (X)	MF	54.3	75.7	39
	M	46.4	62.7	35

[a] Males and females.
[b] Males.

TABLE 47
Rajasthan, Educational Development, 1957–1961

Grade	Sex	Enrollment (in Thousands)		Percentage Increase,
		1957	1961	1957–61
Grade I	MF [a]	225	455	102
	M [b]	182	362	99
Grade II	MF	133	227	71
	M	111	183	65
Last grade of primary level (V)	MF	67.1	111	65
	M	58.1	91.8	58
First grade of middle level (VI)	MF	51.2	87.4	71
	M	45.3	74.7	65
Last grade of middle level (VIII)	MF	35.1	52.0	48
	M	31.6	45.9	45
First grade of high school level (IX)	MF	24.8	38.9	57
	M	22.8	35.2	54
Last full grade of high school level (X)	MF	19.5	30.7	57
	M	18.1	28.0	55

[a] Males and females.
[b] Males.

TABLE 48
Uttar Pradesh, Educational Development, 1957–1961

Grade	Sex	Enrollment (in Thousands)		Percentage Increase,
		1957	1961	1957–61
Grade I	MF [a]	1,102	1,467	33
	M [b]	865	1,129	31
Grade II	MF	647	912	41
	M	513	716	40
Last grade of primary level (V)	MF	338	438	30
	M	287	357	24
First grade of middle level (VI)	MF	231	313	36
	M	202	263	30
Last grade of middle level (VIII)	MF	195	244	25
	M	176	212	20
First grade of high school level (IX)	MF	149	176	18
	M	136	156	15
Last full grade of high school level (X)	MF	135	182	35
	M	125	163	31

[a] Males and females.
[b] Males.

TABLE 49

West Bengal, Educational Development, 1957–1961

Grade	Sex	Enrollment (in Thousands)		
		1957	1961	Percentage Increase, 1957–61
Grade I	MF [a]	1,139	1,256	10
	M [b]	701	764	9.0
Grade II	MF	522	603	16
	M	354	391	10
Last grade of primary level (IV)	MF	293	399	36
	M	214	238	11
First grade of middle level (V)	MF	193	250	30
	M	156	180	15
Last grade of middle level (VIII)	MF	108	141	31
	M	86	107	24
First grade of high school level (IX)	MF	90.8	114	26
	M	75.1	89.6	19
Last full grade of high school level (X)	MF	62.4	80.2	29
	M	50.4	63.7	26

[a] Males and females.
[b] Males.

the states identified do not coincide exactly with either the grouping based on enrollments by level or by terminal grade.

According to the verbal statements of priorities expressed in the plans, all of the states except Kerala and possibly Orissa would have been expected to give principal attention to the expansion of primary education during the second plan period. Yet, as these tables show, this order of priority existed in only a limited number of states. The actual priorities for educational development that were followed in the states, therefore, generally conformed to the reversed order of emphasis that has been revealed in the analysis of national statistics.

VI

Conclusions

The basic finding that emerges from this study is one that appears to have critical importance for the concept of formal national educational planning: India has not been able to implement a relatively optimal educational plan, in spite of the fact that the responsible educational authorities seem to have been aware of the nation's basic quantitative educational requirements. In this chapter, the evidence for this conclusion will be summarized. Some possible explanations for this finding will also be briefly discussed and suggestions for further research presented.

Summary of the Evidence

Through the use of several simplifying assumptions and the analysis of data from the educational experience of other countries, it has been possible to hypothesize for the purposes of this investigation that India's quantitative educational requirements during the present stage of its educational development entail (1) a limitation of the expansion of general secondary and university education, and (2) the attainment of universal primary schooling. This interpretation of India's educational needs is supported by the widespread unemployment and the inappropriate employment of highly educated persons, and by the acknowledgment of the country's highest educational officials that excessive quantities of general secondary and university education have been provided. At the same time, the need to achieve universal primary schooling has been officially recognized and embodied in the provisions of Article 45 of the Indian Constitution.

Formal national educational planning in India began with the publication of the plan of the Central Advisory Board of Education in 1944. A supplement to this plan—the Kher Committee Report—was published in 1950. During 1951–1961, three national five-year plans were prepared, each of which contains a chapter devoted to the projected development of the general educational system. With the exception of the CABE Plan and the secondary education section of the First Five-Year Plan, all of the plans advocate in their texts a course of educational development that conforms to the country's quantitative educational requirements: restricted growth of general education at the secondary and university levels, and the attainment of universal primary schooling. But it cannot be affirmed that India has been able to formulate and adopt a relatively optimal educational plan, for in addition to the verbal statements of desired developmental priorities the plans also present specific quantitative targets for the primary and secondary levels. The orders of priority implicit in the quantitative targets of the first two five-year plans involve approximately equivalent rates of expansion for the primary and secondary levels and, in the Third Five-Year Plan, an actual reversal of the verbal statement of priorities. Only in the CABE Plan and the Kher Committee Report is there no contradiction between the two sets of priorities.

An examination of the growth of the Indian school system during 1950–1961 reveals that the orders of priority given in the verbal statements of the plans have in fact been reversed during the course of implementation. Thus, even the specific quantitative targets of the first and second five-year plans have not been achieved, since they postulated approximately equivalent rates of expansion for the primary and secondary levels. The growth of the various state school systems during 1957–1961 also generally conformed to the pattern for India as a whole, with most of the states showing an inversion of the planned priorities.[1]

The Failure of Implementation: Possible Explanations

When the targets of a plan are not achieved, one or more of the following causal factors are indicated: (1) the goals may not have been accepted by the individuals or groups responsible for plan im-

---

[1] It must be emphasized that the limitations adopted for this study in order to render the subject manageable have precluded an analysis of India's qualitative educational requirements. It might well be argued, therefore, that before any expansion of primary schooling took place, the most optimal utilization of available resources would necessitate an improvement in the quality of general secondary and university education. However, the interpretation of India's quantitative educational requirements presented in this investigation does not rule out this course of action; it only attempts to stipulate objectives that would be appropriate if and when quantitative development is warranted.

Similarly, India's educational plans might also have been examined from the point of view of other criteria than the priorities for educational development. For example, the plans might have been considered on the basis of the means available for their implementation and the extent to which limitations in resources were realistically perceived. Such an evaluation might have shown the CABE Plan to be superior to the Kher Committee Report, even though the latter contained a more appropriate order of priorities than the former.

plementation, with the result that no attempt was made to carry out the plan; (2) the means specified or assumed in the plan may not have been the ones used to implement the plan, and thus plan objectives were not reached, although they might have been attained if the correct means had been employed; or (3) the means specified or assumed in the plan may have been technically deficient and incapable of bringing about the desired results. Hence, until investigations are conducted to identify the particular causes involved, it will not be possible to provide a completely satisfactory exposition of the reasons why India's educational plans have not been successfully implemented. Nevertheless, some of the principal factors relevant to an interpretation of this failure seem to be obvious, and thus warrant at least brief discussion.

The non-attainment of universal primary schooling does not appear to have been due to the inaccessibility of primary schools. According to the All-India Educational Survey of 1957, 83.1 percent of the population resided within one mile of a primary school.[2] By 1963 the situation was even more favorable; all six replies received in response to a questionnaire addressed to the educational ministers of the states by the present author during the course of this investigation reported that educational facilities at the primary level were accessible to nearly every child of school age.[3] The main obstacles to the attainment of universal primary schooling, therefore, seem to be social and economic. As the Madras *White Paper on Education* has pointed out,

> . . . now that 'Schoollessness' has been reduced to very small proportions, it may be taken that the main factor at work is poverty. Not less than one-third of all the parents in the State seem to be at least indifferent, often unwilling, to send children to school, even though it is within easy reach and no fees are charged.[4]

Even the small contribution that children can make to the family livelihood is regarded as sufficient reason for parents to keep them at home rather than send them to school, which could also necessitate a significant outlay on clothing and books. The answer to this problem would seem to be to offer incentives (such as the provision of free school lunches) for school attendance that will compensate parents

[2] India, Ministry of Education, *Report of the All-India Educational Survey* (Delhi: Manager of Publications, 1960), p. 484. West Bengal did not participate in this survey.

[3] Because of the confidential nature of the replies obtained, the respondents will not be further identified.

[4] Madras State, *White Paper on Education* (1956), p. 33.

for the loss of their children's services. Programs of this type, however, would require additional governmental expenditures; and with the continued expansion of the higher levels of the school system, adequate resources do not seem to be available for the primary level.

The inability to control the growth of secondary and university level education is, therefore, another major factor responsible for the non-implementation of India's educational plans. In accounting for this expansion—which, according to the verbal statements of priorities in the plans, should have been minimal at most—the possibility of the means specified or assumed in the plans being deficient or not utilized does not arise, since the decision to maintain stable enrollments at the post-primary levels would not entail any means for effective implementation. The fact that enrollments at the post-primary levels have increased can, therefore, be explained as resulting from the non-acceptance of the objectives of the plans by the implementing agency.

In the questionnaire survey referred to above, four of the six replies from the state governments indicated that no attempt was made to control the expansion of the post-primary levels of the school system. One of the replies contained the following statement: "There is no check on the enrollment at any stage [level] by any authority." Another response affirmed that while "provision [in the plans] does not exist for Secondary and Collegiate Education it is not proposed to discourage popular enthusiasm." [5]

Indeed, as the recent *Report of the Education Commission: 1964– 66* seems to indicate, it is doubtful whether the Government of India can any longer even formulate a relatively optimal educational plan. Although the Education Commission declared that the "most crucial" requirement is "to provide, as directed by Article 45 of the Constitution, free and compulsory education of good quality to all children," the existence of a strong "public demand" for education at the secondary and university levels was also acknowledged. The Commission went on to admit that heretofore this public demand had been accommodated as follows: ". . . access to all secondary education was provided on an open-door basis; and in higher education, both the selective and open-door policies were operated upon simultaneously in different sectors." In giving its advice for the planning of secondary level enrollments during the period 1966–1986, the Commission cau-

---

[5] It is sometimes argued in justification of the unrestricted expansion of post-primary schooling that the limitation of educational opportunities is undemocratic. While it is not within the scope of this investigation to consider the ethical issues involved, it may well be asked whether relegating an individual to a life of illiteracy by failing to provide primary schooling is less undemocratic than withholding the privilege of post-primary schooling from a person who has not been selected for admission to a secondary school.

tioned that "the pressures of expansion will increase rather than decrease because of such factors as . . . the spread of the desire for post-elementary education to all sections of society." Accordingly, the Commission postulated an increase of approximately 100 percent in the total enrollment of grades VIII–X during 1966–1976, while it suggested that enrollments in grades I–IV should increase by only about 65 percent in the same period.[6] If in making these proposals the Education Commission was showing a realistic awareness of the politics of Indian education, it also appeared to be rejecting the possibility of ever producing and implementing the kind of educational plan which would maximize societal benefits.

Suggestions for Further Research

This analysis of educational planning in India has thus returned to the fundamental problem which was posed at the beginning of the investigation: whether the preparation and implementation of a relatively optimal educational plan is a practical possibility in any developing society. It has been shown that the preparation of such a plan in India was feasible, at least at one time. But as this case study also demonstrates, the implementation of India's educational plans has not resulted in a pattern of quantitative educational development that accords with the verbal statements of priority put forward in those plans.

Most of the research effort in the field of educational planning undertaken by the international organizations and the U. S. Agency for International Development has been directed toward the improvement of the techniques of formal planning. This focus would be justified if the principal reason for a nation's departing from a relatively optimal course of educational development is ignorance of what this course should be. But if the conclusions reached in the present study are applicable to other countries than India (as seems very likely to be true), it is evident that much greater attention needs to be given to the problem of what happens to a relatively optimal plan once it has been formulated. Further research is particularly required, therefore, on the process of educational decision-making in order to elucidate the factors which affect the adoption and implementation of relatively optimal educational plans. Such studies are essential if formal planning is to become an effective instrument of educational development.

[6] India, Ministry of Education, *Report of the Education Commission: 1964–66* (Delhi: Manager of Publications, 1966), pp. 90–91, 161, 166–167.

Bibliography and sources of information

Bibliography

Public Documents: India

Avinashilingam, T. S. *Gandhiji's Experiments in Education.* Delhi: Manager of Publications, 1960.

Census of India: 1951. Paper No. 3 of 1954: *Age Tables.*

Census of India: 1961. Paper No. 1 of 1962: *Final Population Totals.*

Census of India: 1961. Paper No. 2 of 1963: *Age Tables.*

Educational Expenditure in India (1950–51 to 1960–61). New Delhi: National Council of Educational Research & Training, 1965.

India. Bureau of Education. *Post-War Educational Development in India.* A Report by the Central Advisory Board of Education, January, 1944. 5th ed. Delhi: Manager of Publications, 1947.

India. Directorate General of Employment and Training. *Report on the Pattern of Graduate Employment.* New Delhi: Directorate General of Employment and Training, 1963. (Draft; mimeographed.)

India. Ministry of Education. *Central Advisory Board of Education (1935–1960): Silver Jubilee Souvenir.* Delhi: Manager of Publications, 1960.

————. *Directory of Institutions for Higher Education: 1961.* Delhi: Manager of Publications, 1961.

————. *Draft Third Five Year Plan for Education.* 1960.

————. *Education in India.* (Vols. for *1950–1959.*)

————. *Education in the States.* (Vols. for *1950–1960.*)

————. *Education in Universities in India.* (Vols. for *1950–1958.*)

————. *Indian University Administration.* Delhi: Manager of Publications, 1958.

————. *A Plan for Secondary Education.* Delhi: Manager of Publications, 1955.

————. *Proceedings of the Educational Conference held at New Delhi in January, 1948.* Delhi: Manager of Publications, 1949.

————. *Proceedings of the Second [Fourth] State Education Ministers' Conference.* Delhi: Manager of Publications, 1960.

————. *Proceedings of the [Third] State Education Ministers' Conference.* Delhi: Manager of Publications, 1958.

————. *Provisional Educational Statistics (as on 31st March, 1962).* New Delhi: Ministry of Education, 1962.

————. *Provisional Statistics of Education in the States, 1960–61.* New Delhi: Ministry of Education, 1963.

121

————. *Report of the All-India Educational Survey.* Delhi: Manager of Publications, 1960.

————. *Report of the Committee on Emotional Integration.* Delhi: Manager of Publications, 1962.

————. *Report of the Committee on the Ways and Means of Financing Educational Development in India.* Delhi: Manager of Publications, 1950.

————. *Report of the Education Commission: 1964–66.* Delhi: Manager of Publications, 1966.

————. *Report of the Secondary Education Commission.* 4th reprint ed. Delhi: Manager of Publications, 1958.

————. *The Report of the University Education Commission (December 1948–August 1949).* 1st reprint ed. Delhi: Manager of Publications, 1963.

————. *Reports of the Committees Appointed by the Central Advisory Board of Education in India (1938–43).* Delhi: Manager of Publications, 1958.

India. Planning Commission. *The First Five Year Plan.* 1952.

————. *Second Five Year Plan.* 1956.

————. *Third Five Year Plan.* Delhi: Manager of Publications, 1961.

————. *Outline Report of the Study Group on Educated Unemployed.* Delhi: Manager of Publications, 1956.

India. *University Grants Commission Act.* 1956.

Madras State. *White Paper on Education.* 1956.

Naik, J. P. *Some Papers on a National System of Education for India.* New Delhi: India, Education Commission, 1965.

Pant, Pitambar, and Chaudhuri, T. P. *Educated Persons in India: 1955.* Delhi: Manager of Publications, 1959.

Report of the Advisory Planning Board, December, 1946. Delhi: Manager of Publications, 1947.

Report of the Legislature Committee on White Paper on Education, Madras State, 1956. Madras: Superintendent, Government Press, 1958.

Other Books and Documents

Alexander-Frutschi, Marian C. (ed.) *Human Resources and Economic Growth: An International Annotated Bibliography on the Role of Education and Training in Economic and Social Development.* Menlo Park, Calif.: Stanford Research Institute, 1963.

Anderson, Ronald S. *Japan: Three Epochs of Modern Education.* (U.S. Office of Education, Bulletin 1959, No. 11.) Washington: Government Printing Office, 1959.

Arrow, Kenneth J. *Social Choice and Individual Values.* New York: John Wiley and Sons, 1951.

Blaug, Mark. *Economics of Education: A Selected Annotated Bibliography.* Oxford: Pergamon Press, 1966.

Bowen, William G. *Economic Aspects of Education: Three Essays.* Princeton: Industrial Relations Section, Princeton University, 1964.

Bowles, Frank. *Access to Higher Education.* Vol. I: *Director's Report.* Paris: UNESCO and the International Association of Universities, 1963.

Buchanan, James M. and Tulloch, Gordon. *The Calculus of Consent.* Ann Arbor: University of Michigan Press, 1962.

Commonwealth Universities Yearbook: 1963. London: Association of Universities of the British Commonwealth, 1963.

DeWitt, Nicholas. *Education and Professional Employment in the USSR.* Washington: Government Printing Office, 1961.

Digest of Educational Statistics. (U.S. Office of Education, Bulletin 1963, No. 43.) Washington: Government Printing Office, 1963.

Downs, Anthony. *An Economic Theory of Democracy.* New York: Harper and Brothers, 1957.

Educational Planning: A Bibliography. Paris: International Institute for Educational Planning, 1964.

Friedman, Milton. *Capitalism and Freedom.* Chicago: University of Chicago Press, 1962.

Hanson, A. H. *The Process of Planning: A Study of India's Five-Year Plans, 1950–1964.* London: Oxford University Press, 1966.

Harbison, Frederick, and Myers, Charles A. *Education, Manpower and Economic Growth.* New York: McGraw-Hill, 1964.

Hitch, Charles J., and McKean, Roland N. *The Economics of Defense in the Nuclear Age.* Cambridge: Harvard University Press, 1960.

International Bureau of Education and UNESCO. *Educational Planning.* Geneva and Paris, 1962.

Kabir, Humayun. *Education in New India.* 2nd ed. London: George Allen and Unwin, 1959.

Kamat, A. R., and Deshmukh, A. G. *Wastage in College Education.* Bombay: Asia Publishing House, 1963.

Krishnamachari, V. T. *Fundamentals of Planning in India.* Bombay: Orient Longmans, 1962.

Kotschnig, Walter. *Unemployment in the Learned Professions: An International Study of Occupational and Educational Planning.* London: Oxford University Press, 1937.

Levy, Marion J. *The Structure of Society.* Princeton: Princeton University Press, 1952.

March, James G., and Simon, Herbert A. *Organizations.* New York: John Wiley and Sons, 1958.

McCully, Bruce T. *English Education and the Origins of Indian Nationalism.* New York: Columbia University Press, 1940.

McKean, Roland N. *Efficiency in Government through Systems Analysis.* New York: John Wiley and Sons, 1958.

National Planning Committee. *Education.* Bombay: Vora and Co., 1948.

Nehru, Jawaharlal. *Discovery of India.* New York: John Day, 1946.

Nurullah, Syed, and Naik, J. P. *History of Education in India during the British Period.* Bombay: Macmillan, 1943.

OECD, *Resources of Scientific and Technical Personnel in the OECD Area.* Paris: OECD, 1963.

Pylee, M. V. *Constitutional Government in India.* Bombay: Asia Publishing House, 1960.

Parnes, Herbert. *Forecasting Educational Needs for Economic and Social Development.* Paris: OECD, 1962.

Passin, Herbert. *Society and Education in Japan.* New York: Teachers College Press, Columbia University, 1965.

Saiyidain, K. G., and Gupta, H. C. *Access to Higher Education in India.* A Report Prepared for the International Study of University Admissions. New Delhi, 1962.

Simon, Herbert A. *Administrative Behavior.* New York: Macmillan, 1948.

Tinbergen, Jan. *Central Planning.* New Haven: Yale University Press, 1964.

UNESCO. *Manual of Educational Statistics.* Paris: UNESCO, 1961.

UNESCO. *World Survey of Education.* Vol. III: *Secondary Education.* Paris: UNESCO, 1961.

UNESCO. *World Survey of Education.* Paris: UNESCO, 1955.

Vaizey, John. *The Economics of Education.* London: Faber & Faber, 1962.

Articles

Anderson, C. Arnold and Bowman, Mary Jean. "Theoretical Considerations in Educational Planning," in *Educational Planning,* ed. Don Adams (Syracuse: Syracuse University Press, 1964), pp. 4–46.

Balogh, Thomas. "The Economics of Educational Planning: Sense and Nonsense," *Comparative Education,* I, No. 1 (October, 1964), 5–17.

Bowman, Mary Jean. "Perspectives on Education and Development," *International Development Review,* VI, No. 3 (September, 1964), 3–7.

————. "Social Returns to Education," *International Social Science Journal,* XIV, No. 4 (1962), 647–659.

Cutts, Elmer H. "The Background of Macaulay's Minute," *American Historical Review,* LVIII (July, 1953), 824–853.

Debeauvais, Michel. "The Balance between the Different Levels of Education," in *The Economics of Education,* ed. E. A. G. Robinson and J. E. Vaizey (New York: St. Martin's Press, 1966), pp. 523–546.

Eckhaus, Richard S. "Education and Economic Growth," in *Economics of Higher Education,* ed. Selma J. Mushkin (Washington: U.S. Government Printing Office, 1962), pp. 647–659.

Hayward, Beresford. "The Implemented Educational Plan," in *Educational Planning,* ed. Don Adams (Syracuse: Syracuse University Press, 1964), pp. 82–102.

Laska, John A. "The Stages of Educational Development," *Comparative Education Review,* VIII, No. 3 (1964), 251–263.

————. "The Use of the 'Educational Pyramid' in Comparative Education," *International Review of Education,* XI (No. 4, 1965), 485–488.

Mukerji, S. N. "States and Education," in *Administration of Education in India,* ed. S. N. Mukerji (Baroda: Acharya Book Depot, 1962), pp. 75–100.

Rivlin, Alice M. "Research in the Economics of Higher Education," in *Economics of Higher Education,* ed. Selma J. Mushkin (Washington: U.S. Government Printing Office, 1962), pp. 360–378.

Saxe, Jo W. "Some Question about the Economics of Education," in *Planning Education for Economic and Social Development,* ed. Herbert S. Parnes (Paris: OECD, 1963), pp. 49–55.

Sen, S. R. "Planning Machinery in India," *Indian Journal of Public Administration,* VII (1961), 215–235.

Sources of Information

Table	Source
1	*Census of India: 1961*, Paper No. 1 of 1962: *Final Population Totals*, Table I.
2	India, Ministry of Education, *Education in India: 1957–58* (Delhi: Manager of Publications, 1962), I, Tables 18, 39, 51, 62.
3	*Educational Expenditure in India (1950–51 to 1960–61)* (New Delhi: National Council of Educational Research and Training, 1965), Table 4 (1).
4	*Educational Expenditure in India (1950–51 to 1960–61)*, Tables 7C, 7E, 8A, 9F.
5	India, Ministry of Education, *Report of the Committee on Emotional Integration* (Delhi: Manager of Publications, 1962), Appendix 16, supplemented by data supplied by the Union Ministry of Education.
6	*Report of the Committee on Emotional Integration*, Appendix 17, supplemented by data supplied by the Union Ministry of Education.
7	India, Ministry of Education, *Education in the States, 1959–1960* (Delhi: Manager of Publications, 1962); *Provisional Statistics of Education in the States, 1960–61* (New Delhi: Ministry of Education, 1963); *Report of the Committee on Emotional Integration*, Appendix 17.
8	Data supplied by the Union Ministry of Education.
9	J. P. Naik, *Some Papers on a National System of Education for India* (New Delhi: India, Education Commission, 1965), Paper No. 3, Annexure 4, Table 2.
10	J. P. Naik, *op. cit.*, Paper No. 3, Annexure 4, Table 2.

Table	Source
11–12	Source as given for Table 10 above, supplemented by data from the Union Ministry of Education and the state education departments.
13	Source as given in Table 10, above.
14	Data supplied by the Union Ministry of Education.
15	Adapted from OECD, *Resources of Scientific and Technical Personnel in the OECD Area* (Paris: OECD, 1963), Table 1, p. 31.
16	Author's compilation.
17	Population data from *Census of India: 1961*, Paper No. 2 of 1963; Age Tables; educational data from Union Ministry of Education and state education departments.
18	Sources as given for Table 17, above.
19	Plan documents.
20	Plan documents.
21	Data supplied by the Education Division, Planning Commission.
22–23	Third Five-Year Plan.
24	Statistical reports of the Union Ministry of Education; unpublished data supplied by the Union Ministry of Education.
25	University Grants Commission, *University Development in India: Interim Report*, Part I, 1962–1963.
26	Educational statistics from reports of the Union Ministry of Education; unpublished data supplied by the Union Ministry of Education. Population statistics from *Census of India: 1951*, Paper No. 3 of 1954: *Age Tables; Census of India: 1961*, Paper No. 2 of 1963: *Age Tables;* 1956 data by interpolation.
27	Statistical reports of the Union Ministry of Education, unpublished data supplied by the Union Ministry of Education.
28	Statistics of enrollments and outputs from reports of the Union Ministry of Education, unpublished data supplied by the Union Ministry of Education.

Table	Source
29	Sources as given for Table 26, above.
30	Sources as given for Table 28, above.
31	Sources as given for Table 27, above.
32	Statistical reports of the Union Ministry of Education; unpublished data supplied by the Union Ministry of Education and the state education departments.
33	See sources of Table 32, above.
34	See sources for Table 27, above.
35–42	See sources for Table 32, above.
43	Unpublished data supplied by the state department of education.
44–45	See sources for Tables 27, above.
46	See sources for Table 32, above.
47–49	See sources for Table 27, above.